AF540837

GLOBAL SYNTHESIS OF EDUCATIONAL ASSESSMENT

GLOBAL SYNTHESIS OF EDUCATIONAL ASSESSMENT

Editor

Dr. Digumarti Bhaskara Rao

M.Sc., M.A., M.A., M.Ed., Ph. D.

R.V.R. College of Education

Srinivasa Nagar Colony

Guntur

Andhra Pradesh

India

DISCOVERY PUBLISHING HOUSE

NEW DELHI

Contents

1

Introduction

The World Conference on Education for All held in 1990 in Jomtien, Thailand, marked a new start in the global quest to universalise basic education and eradicate illiteracy. Through the Jomtien Declaration and the Framework for Action, commitments were made and directions set for a decade of large-scale and sustained efforts. Agreements were entered into by countries, inter-governmental organisations, and NGOs to work together throughout the decade. The EFA Forum was established to guide and coordinate the work, to monitor progress and to assess achievements.

Further global and regional conferences throughout the 90s reinforced the Jomtien message, setting it in a global context of social and economic development and environmental change. Several cooperative ventures were launched in order to monitor student learning achievements, to share knowledge and experience and to drive the Jomtien agenda forward.

Throughout the decade countries have introduced a wide array of educational reforms either directly within or related to the six target dimensions agreed at Jomtien. In preparation for the World Conference to be held in Dakar in April 2000, the progress that countries have made and the difficulties and setbacks they have encountered have been analysed in a series of national reports, regional synthesis reports, thematic studies, and other documents. The material is presented according to the six target dimensions.

Countries in their pursuit of the Jomtien goals were invited to set their own specific targets according to their situations and capabilities. Thus there are many country-specific differences in the kinds of material that have been prepared, the topics that have been treated and the issues that have been identified. The Jomtien Declaration was grounded in fundamental values and principles, several of which proved extremely difficult for a number of countries to sustain. This Report attempts to capture that diversity of response, within as well as between countries. Consequently quite varied kinds of evidence are drawn upon.

The 'Jomtien decade' witnessed important contextual changes both positive and negative for the achievement of the EFA goals: the collapse of political regimes, civil war, scientific and technological advances, major economic fluctuations, and others. These changes had quite different impacts on different countries and regions.

Analysis of the success or otherwise countries have had in achieving the Jomtien goals forms the main body of this Global Synthesis. For each of the six target dimensions, an account is rendered, based largely on the materials prepared for the EFA 2000 Assessment and drawing on the judgements of this authors.

Arising from experience in trying to achieve their targets, a number of cross-cutting issues have emerged.

- how to overcome barriers to improved access and greater equity;
- strengthening the quality, relevance and effectiveness of education;
- new patterns of shared responsibility and decision-taking;
- ways to mobilise resources and use the more effectively;
- the creation of a new educational knowledge base.

What have been the results of the EFA movement? What are its major success, its shortcomings and failures? Have the goals been attained? What has been learnt and how can the experience of the Jomtien decade be used for the design and development of the next stage?

Answers to these questions are given, but they are neither simple nor straightforward. Partly this is because of large variations in the quantity and quality of information that has been provided. Also, answers are inevitably complex, given the breadth of the target dimensions and the different courses countries have taken in the definition and pursuit of their own targets. Trend analysis in particular is not possible in any systematic way, but snapshots are taken throughout the Report to highlight singular achievements or critical problems. Despite the difficulties of analysis and assessment, overall major gains can be clearly identified as can the shortcomings. The capacity to monitor and evaluate has been greatly enhanced as a direct result of the Jomtien movement and associated developments. This alone counts as a major achievement of great value for future work.

The purpose of target setting is to stimulate creative thinking and planning and to mobilise action. These have certainly occurred on a large scale. Countries have not mechanically followed the Jomtien framework: instead they have interpreted and modified according to their own requirements. This in fact is quite in line with the original agreements. This in fact is quite in line with the original agreements and expectations. The targets were defined as directions to which countries would relate their own goals and strategies. There have been setbacks and failures, including a lack of commitment and leadership, poor planning and management, neglect of critical problems. It cannot be concluded that, from a global perspective, the targets have yet been reached or reached in quite the way they were thought about a decade ago. Nevertheless, in the following ways there has been real progress towards achieving the Jomtien goals:

- Significant improvements in achieving enrolment, and participation targets for basic education at all levels of education including early childhood care and education;
- Big reductions in some countries in inequities, notably in the area of gender, disability and ethnic minorities;
- Big reductions in a small number of countries in volumes and/or rates of adult illiteracy;
- Now policies, frameworks, legislation and resources in several countries to pursue one or more of the EFA target directions;
- Greater involvement of non-government organisations, community groups and parents in decision making, action programmes and the operation of child care and education facilities;
- Big improvements in educational information and in analytic and evaluative capacity (the knowledge base);
- The targets, although not achieved or fully achieved, are more attainable than a decade ago.

Whatever the failures and setbacks, there is more than enough here to demonstrate the massive achievements and value of the EFA movement and to inspire confidence in the future.

2

Setting Directions

At Jomtien, Thailand, in March 1990 representatives of the global education community met in the World Conference on Education for All and embraced a new vision. More than a unique event, this Conference signalled a powerful movement which, while picking up on many threads from the past, sought to weave a strong new fabric.

The World Declaration on Education for All (EFA) adopted at Jomtien went far beyond a renewed commitment to earlier targets set for basic education and adult literacy. It spoke for universal access to education as a fundamental right of all people, for fair and equitable treatment of all learners – infants, children, youth and adults. It underlined the need for better learning environments, for new partnerships, for improved quality in educational procedures and results – and for both more resources and improvements in resource utilisation.

Together with the accompanying Framework for Action to Meet Basic Learning Needs, also adopted at Jomtien, the World Declaration on EFA set goals and priorities. Strategies were adopted which would tie commitment to action, mobilising all possible resources.

It was a remarkable achievement for the world education community to reach this policy consensus and agree on the set of aspirational goals. The Jomtien agreements and decisions outlined broad programmatic directions designed to substantially improve opportunities and raise the level of educational performance in all countries. For the first time, there was a framework which, however ambitious, set clear directions for purposive worldwide action.

Preparation for the Jomtien World Conference involved agreements among UNICEF, UNDP, UNESCO and the World Bank, subsequently joined by UNFPA, and included nine regional consultations. In 1991, following the World Conference, an International Consultative Forum on Education for All (referred to hereafter as the EFA Forum) was established. Its mandate was to 'serve national follow-up action and support it effectively' and 'seek to maintain the spirit of co-operation amongst countries, multilateral and bilateral agencies, as well as NGOs.'

The EFA Forum was conceived as a series of global meetings for the EFA partners to discuss progress, and matters of mutual concern. Also established for operational purposes were a Forum Secretariat and a Forum Steering Committee, and subsequently, a Management Committee. Of signal importance is the widely representative nature of the EFA Forum, a unique global mechanism of consultation and co-operation among countries, multilateral and bilateral development agencies, non-governmental organisations, the private sector and media.

A preliminary meeting in Paris in 1991 was followed by one in Delhi in 1993, when nine of the world's most populous countries and some others, together with donor countries and agencies, established a working alliance of developing countries with large populations – the E9 initiative. These countries have met regularly at ministerial level, for collaborative action and information sharing.

At Amman, Jordan, the world education community met again in 1996, to review progress and to pinpoint the major obstacles still in the way. Regional meetings and data gathering preceded the Amman Meeting. Four issues that have persisted since were raised: the need to balance quality learning with the attention being given to years of schooling; concerns over the quality of data; insufficient recognition of the activities of non-governmental organisations; and the need to maintain the EFA momentum at country and regional levels.

Now, in preparation for this World Conference in Dakar a decade of achievements, difficulties and remaining barriers has been comprehensively documented, analysed and appraised. Countries have been grouped into transnational regions by the EFA Forum and syntheses prepared to point up trends and issues, region by region. A most impressive, indeed unprecedented, body of information on world education is the result. In a wealth of national reports, regional and sub-regional syntheses, thematic studies and a statistical document, masses of both quantitative and qualitative data have been assembled and reviewed. Trends have been defined and developments and setbacks reported. Gaps and deficiencies have been frankly addressed. Significant issues have been raised for further consideration.

The time has now come to pull these strands together. It is impossible to do justice to the richness of all this material in a 'global synthesis'. Necessarily this Report is highly selective, focusing on main trends, major issues and examples to illustrate key points.

Not to be overlooked in reviewing the decade is the substantial growth and refinement of knowledge about education trends and the conditions which either enable or inhibit attainment of the goals that have been set. At the outset this major achievement in capacity building, analytic power and understanding must be acknowledged and warmly welcomed. The Education For All movement has likewise demonstrated the value of global collaboration through the EFA Forum.

Much has been learned from the experience of addressing the Jomtien agenda on the ground and from the processes of analysis and evaluation of results. There is a clearer understanding now both of what the Jomtien commitments actually meant in practice and of the nature of the challenges that they posed. A firm platform has been established for future action.

The basic messages of Jomtien remain, but adjustments, elaborations and further undertakings based on the experience of the past decade are now called for. The Dakar World Education Forum together with its Framework for Action, in providing the opportunity for a strongly renewed commitment to practical action, also enables new targets to be met.

Many different routes can be tracked from Jomtien to Dakar, as countries reached towards the goals and values of Education for All. Differences of culture, tradition, environment, social, political and economic conditions and educational systems have profoundly influenced the ways countries went about achieving the Jomtien goals, and their rates of progress. A key issue is the level of commitment, and leadership, resourcefulness and determination in face of the challenges.

There have been failures and setbacks, stagnation as well as progress, and these must be put in the balance. Overall, the studies and appraisals that have been made of the decade of effort since Jomtien both underline the need and give renewed hope for the continuing development of education worldwide. We can again unite in determining future directions and continuing responsible action to achieve the goals.

The extent to which the Jomtien decade has been a success in achieving the targets set in 1990 is the subject of the overall EFA 2000 Assessment of which this Global Synthesis forms part. 'Success' has been variously defined, since countries were expected to work within a framework, setting their own targets. In many countries these targets were reached or sometimes exceeded; in others there are very big shortfalls. 'Success' in these circumstances requires interpretation from many different standpoints as well as complex judgements about a large and varied body of data.

There Have Been Major Achievements

In three quite clear ways, as a process, the 'Jomtien decade' can be deemed a success:

1) Mobilising global action to improve education;
2) Developing the knowledge base and analytic capacity;
3) Identifying and clarifying the areas requiring further concerted action.

But...

1) commitment and involvement have been uneven,
2) not all targets have been pursued with the necessary vigour.
3) despite the overall improvements, in some countries education reform stood still during the 90s or there have been declines.

3

The 'Jomtien Decade'

PRINCIPLES AND PURPOSE

The commitments and undertakings made at Jomtien were premised on quite fundamental values and beliefs:

- People everywhere have basic human aspirations and needs: these include nurture, health, training and education in order to fulfil themselves and live well in their families, their communities and as citizens;
- injustice, poverty, disease, war and violence are inimical to the satisfaction of basic human needs;
- All societies have fundamental requirements and they have obligations towards all their members, whose rights as affirmed in the Universal Declaration of Human Rights include education;
- There is a bond between people and society of mutual rights, responsibilities, duties and commitments; education serves to strengthen and enrich this bond.

The movement of Education for All (from Jomtien to Dakar and beyond) affirms:

- The right of all people everywhere to basic education;
- People's needs and responsibilities as learners;
- Society's expectations and requirements of its members as learners;
- The need for commitment, leadership and change in the education environment and wider context to foster and facilities learning.

The overriding purpose of the global movement of education for all is no less than the achievement of a better life for all people, grounded in civilised values and human rights and responsibilities. The goals set and the strategies adopted have, as their rationale, global agreements and commitments to make a living reality of a vision. That reality, however, must embody and express the principles underlying the Jomtien Declaration and Framework for Action.

These principles are ethical, humane and civic; they are culturally and socially sensitive. Mutual obligations and responsibilities bind people and communities together. They can be described as a set of social virtues; combining goodness with efficiency. These virtues include: equity and justice; fairness; empathy and considerateness; peace; the valuing of difference; and active democratic citizenship. They combine in the ideal of a full, good life for everyone, to which education ministers.

Have learning opportunities for all people everywhere—infants, children, youth and adults-been provided? For the EFA 2000 Assessment, there are questions to raise about rates of progress and the directions pursued in achieving the goals. As these questions are addressed, it is also necessary to ask how far and in what ways have equity, justice, peace, and democracy been advanced.

THE SIX DIMENSIONS OF THE JOMTIEN TARGETS FOR EDUCATION

Achieving universal basic education poses very different

challenges for different countries and regions and for particular groups within countries. Even so, it was agreed that there could be a common set of target directions for all countries. Countries were invited at Jomtien to set their targets for the 1990s in terms of six dimensions.

Countries have provided data for each of these targets which have been analysed in reports on each major regional grouping: Asia and the Pacific; the Americas; Arab States and North Africa; Europe; Sub-Saharan Africa; E9 (the nine most populous countries).

These targets have been operationalised and analysed in the Statistical Document, through 18 core EFA indicators. These indicators are designed to describe and measure the main components of basic education as envisaged and agreed at Jomtien, and progress over the decade. Despite the active encouragement and support to countries and EFA regions to provide data through these 18 indicators as well as in many other ways, there are, inevitably, many gaps. In the statistical data and in the country and EFA regional reports there are considerable variations in coverage and topics discussed. A set of highly authoritative special thematic studies, commissioned by intergovernmental organisations and NGOs, draws upon statistical data, surveys, the research literature, anecdotal evidence and other sources in providing rich insights and judgements about trends and issues that lie at the heart of the EFA movement. A number of reports on specific topics and projects have been prepared, including information on student performance in several reports on the UNESCO-UNICEF project, Monitoring Learning Achievement (MLA). But despite freely acknowledged deficiencies, the knowledge base is vastly better in 2000 than 1990.

THE WIDE JOMTIEN AGENDA

The suggested target directions and hence the statistical indicators are part of a larger framework of concepts, ideals and ideas, and strategies of action which were incorporated into the Jomtien Declaration and Framework for Action. The key concepts of learning and of learning in different settings and in a variety of modes, were treated in the Jomtien documentation in considerably broader contexts than schooling and the provision of formal education through school-like instrumentalities. Countries have not, however, often reported as comprehensively on learning as was expected.

Other considerations that were raised at Jomtien include; cost effectiveness and improved efficiency; local empowerment and community action; the disabled; partnerships; the terms and conditions of service of teachers; child care and development; education in the context of cross-sectorial policies (economic, trade, labour, employment, health, etc.); and private and voluntary funding sources.

Overall, albeit often implicit, there has been a clear set of expectations for the 90s: improved human development policy; appropriate legislative and regulatory frameworks; well-managed systems and procedures; competent personnel of integrity; transparent and accountable use of resources; enhanced public awareness; and better learning opportunities and outcomes. That in many countries one or more of these expectations could not be met or was not reported, would in no sense be a reason to forego or dilute them in future planning.

...REFLECTING THE TIMES

At Jomtien, attention was frequently drawn to the political, social, economic and cultural environments which both condition educational policies and practices and are interactively informed and modified through education. Satisfaction was expressed over progress (at that time) towards peaceful entente, greater co-operation among nations, the increasing recognition of women's rights and capacities, growth of information services and scientific and cultural developments.

Set against these and other positive trends at the beginning of the 90s were conditions and forces which could jeopardies future progress: mounting debt burdens; threats of economic stagnation and decline; and rapid and unsustainable population growth; widening economic and other disparities within and between countries; war, occupation and civil strife; enforced migration; violent crime; widespread environmental degradation; and the preventable death of millions of children. Especially – but not only – in the lest developed countries these negative forces had resulted in major setbacks to education throughout the 80s.

...BUT THERE ARE EMERGING NEW CONTEXTS

The Jomtien Declaration and Framework for Action were forged in a particular historical setting. Today, a decade later, that context has undergone transformations. In the changing environments of the 90s, topics scarcely considered at Jomtien or developments not anticipated have come to the fore. Their seriousness and impact will require some reshaping of the new agenda and hence of target directions for the next phase of EFA.

To mention only some of the most dramatic changes of the era:

- the political, social and economic shifts in Eastern and Central Europe;
- the rapid development of the Internet as a pervasive lever of change for the organisations of life, commerce, entertainment and education;
- the emerging new economy based on intangible capital and calling for much increased adaptability to rapid change and a new repertoire of entrepreneurial capabilities and attitudes;
- dramatic developments in the life sciences with far-reaching implications;
- the voluntary and enforced movements and mixing of people and cultures.

- the growth of poverty and increasing debt around citadels of increasing affluence; and the swift advance of economic and cultural globalisation.

Whole countries and regions within countries have experienced either economic decline and collapse or unprecedented growth cycles; war zones and areas of civil unrest have spread with whole populations held to ransom; and in some regions, notably Sub-Saharan Africa, there has been the disastrous spread of the HIV/AIDS pandemic. It seems, also, that there has been an intensification of natural disasters attributable to climate change, underlining the need for much improved emergency services.

...AND REINFORCEMENTS OF THE EFA MISSION

Strategic reinforcement of the EFA mission and of the expressed need for further sustained efforts has come from several different sources:

first, the continued growth of systematic knowledge including increased understanding of changes in the wider environment impacting on education;

second, a succession of world conferences throughout the 90s which have both documented and given prominence and publicity to major world issues, many of these having quite direct educational implications (see Appendix); and

third, changes in communication, trade and international finance which heighten public awareness of global interdependence and imbalances.

The advance of educational knowledge and understanding is a particular relevance to the fulfilment of the Jomtien mission. While not an explicit target at Jomtien, knowledge building has in fact proved to be one of its most positive outcomes with highly significant implications for future strategic capability and the ability to target action and mobilise resources.

By the end of the decade, there are much more advanced systems for data collection and analysis in many countries than existed at the beginning. There has been a real effort by the UNESCO Institute for Statistics, working closely with national and other statistical agencies around the world, to come to terms with previously existing deficiencies. Country reports, regional syntheses and the special studies provide numerous examples of improved data sources and advances in knowledge. The problems have not all been solved but they are, at least, much better documented and understood. This should be seen as a crucial step towards overcoming them.

Of course, not all improvements in educational knowledge are attributable to Jomtien, but there have been several important gains consistent with the Jomtien Framework for Action and supportive of its goals. For example, the initiative for the development of an international set of education indicators by the Organisation for Economic Co-operation and Development (OECD) predates Jomtien and has proceeded largely independent of it, has that Organisations's procedures for reviewing educational trends and developments in member countries and others. Likewise, the education statistics work of the European Union (Eurostat), its reviews and those of the Council of Europe and other international bodies are free-standing. They can, however, all be counted as major regional achievements supportive in various ways of the EFA mission. They have a potential extending far beyond the regions in question.

Whether or not specific development programmes, progress in research, and advances in knowledge for decision making are attributable to Jomtien is of far less significance than their strengthening and reinforcing of the broad international movement to improve education and learning.

THE EVOLVING CONCEPT OF BASIC EDUCATION: SCHOOLING, EDUCATION AND LIFELONG LEARNING

In affirming the universal right to and need for education,

the Jomtien Declaration must be interpreted in the broadest possible sense of learning—formal, non-formal and informal—and at any stage of life. Learning takes place in and out of school—in the home, the local community, the workplace, and in recreational and other settings. Not confined to childhood and the formative years, it extends from infancy throughout the whole of life. What is 'basic' is no longer confined to the primary school or formal education. An important achievement of the EFA movement is the closer attention being given especially by NGOs and voluntary bodies to the foundations of learning in the 0-6 period. Care, nurture and encouragement of all round child development at this stage are increasingly being recognised as essential for subsequent growth and hence of satisfactory basic education.

Increasingly, also, there is a challenge to find appropriate structures for supporting and recognising different kinds of learning previously disregarded or given scant recognition in formal education systems. Most countries are still at a relatively early stage in developing new procedures for assessing competence and awarding new kinds of qualifications that give credit for experiential learning that takes place outside formal education institutions. For education of all kinds, there is scope for much greater use of a variety of media and settings and hitherto untapped resources, as pointed out in several of the special studies (1).

The issue of the diversity of learning and the danger of equating 'learning' with 'schooling' having been noted, it remains true that organised schooling provides, for most people, essential foundations for learning over the life-cycle. As many of the country reports point out, schooling builds on a platform of early childhood care and education (ECCE). It is succeeded by vocational preparation, tertiary education and organised adult, continuing education which have reached a highly advanced stage in a growing number of countries. Schools and school teachers are also a resource for adult literacy and continuing education programmes, not only in developing countries where they have a vital role. While there are indispensable, major contributions to education and learning by all kinds of voluntary bodies, community and self-help organisations, however, the provision by public authorities of schools of good quality, access to schools, and opportunities and active encouragement for all to succeed and progress in and through schooling remain the essential and central ingredients of EFA.

The commitment of EFA is to **basic education.** But this is not a fixed or clearcut concept and countries were advised at Jomtien to determine their own definition. Most but by no means all have chosen to restrict 'basic' to primary schooling, meaning the first stage of formal schooling—which so many have yet to attain. 'Basic', in an increasing number of countries, however, now connotes not only early childhood care and education and primary schooling. In some it now encompasses junior secondary schooling and in others it extends to a full secondary education. China, for example, is shifting the focus for much of the country from the primary school to the nine year compulsory school, preceded by a variety of early childhood care and education programmes. The National Education Guidelines and Framework Law in Brazil in 1996 defined the whole system from day care provision to the end of secondary schooling as 'basic'. In Nigeria, 'basic' education refers to early childhood care and pre-primary education, primary schooling and the first three years of secondary. Throughout Europe, North America and Australasia, Japan and parts of South East Asia, 'basic' includes both primary and secondary levels.

In a small but growing number of countries, some kind of post secondary or tertiary education is almost becoming 'basic' in that it is seen as a foundation for working life or further studies for all youth. There are moves to incorporate all levels and forms of education within a framework of 'lifelong learning for all'. These require a reconsideration of just what is best taught and learned in childhood and youth, as a foundation for continuing learning.

Difficult—indeed unnecessary—as it is to maintain clearcut distinctions, for ease of communication as well as target setting, basic education does need to be redefined, with reference to 'technical', 'specialist', 'higher', 'tertiary' and 'lifelong'.

'Basic' in this Report refers to the competencies, knowledge, attitudes, values and motivations that are deemed necessary in order for people to become fully literate and to have developed the educational foundations for a lifelong learning journey. Basic education commences at birth and may be achieved through either formal or non-formal means and agencies. Competencies, skills and substantive learnings defined as basic, when provided for in schools and similar institutions, are usually cast in the form of a core curriculum which while it includes and builds on literacy includes numeracy, social and scientific knowledge, physical and health education and the arts and crafts. Dimensions like visual and aural literacy and oracy—in a world where multi-media are pervasive—are no less 'basic' than verbal and numerical skills. In short, the four 'Delors pillars'—learning to know; learning to do; learning to live together; learning to be—are all basic.(2)

The length and nature of schooling that have been defined as 'basic' by countries vary: from a bare minimum of 3-4 years of primary school to a nine year school, or completion of full secondary schooling. Programmes and campaigns of adult literacy are an example of non-formal basic education, as are community health campaigns, parental education in child care and educational campaigns conducted through the mass media. 'Basic' with reference to these minimum levels, should be treated as the very early stages of a process that needs to continue and grow.

COMMON TARGETS AND DIVERSE CIRCUMSTANCES

As the EFA 2000 Assessment reports indicate, education and especially schooling is firmly grounded in the historical, cultural, social, economic and political conditions of countries and regions within them. These constitute environments, which profoundly affect not only policies, legislation, regulations and resources, but also the quality of the curriculum, the capacity of teachers and the conditions of teaching and learning. Countries are not affected equally, nor are regions, groups, families and individuals within countries.

A question arises therefore as to just how far goals and targets can be described as 'common' when such varied meanings are attached to the term 'basic' and when circumstances for attainment vary so widely, not only between but also within countries. The six target directions were outlined at the beginning of the decade with such generality as to be applicable universally, although with a bias in a couple of them towards countries with low rates of participation and literacy. The translation of these broad general targets into country—and regional-specific policies and programmes was properly left to the countries themselves as was the anticipated rate of progress in attaining them. Thus one of the most problematic aspects of EFA—the pursuit of common goals and the implementation of strategies in circumstances of enormous diversity—must be kept to the fore in assessing the achievements of the Jomtien decade. Inevitably, rates of progress from quite unequal starting points and in a great variety of environments differ dramatically.

While global, regional and national indicators tell important stories, they cannot completely capture either the full range of conditioning factors or the diversity of provision, resource and response within countries. It is by attention to environmental conditions as reported in the variety of documents assessing progress and problems that the diversity can best be understood. Many countries, in responding to the Jomtien challenge and in pursuing their reform strategies, adapted targets to the diverse circumstances. For example, extreme regional inequalities in Brazil have seen the national government in a federal system playing a differentiated provisioning and redistributive role. In China, there are different targets for length of primary schooling in different arts of the country. These presumably would eventually by amalgamated within the overall target of the nine year compulsory school, but that is not at all imminent.

Inevitably much of the concern that has been expressed in the reports of progress since Jomtien relates to the difficulties many countries or parts of countries are experiencing. Making adequate provision for access and participation by learners and for teachers to be adequately prepared, equipped and resourced to carry out their work is still a monumental challenge in many countries and areas. These difficulties reflect conditions and circumstances which in part are beyond the education system itself. Although frequently not open to direct action through educational policies and programmes, they must however be addressed, both as conditions for the realisation of EFA goals and as susceptible over time to influence, if not complete redirection, by a well educated populace. The need for a renewed commitment is evident in those countries where little if any progress has been made.

Educational policies which squarely address the key issues are needed and can work, as has been shown in those countries that are making progress. Educational reform can itself be a potent means for achieving much more effective use of resources and for improving economic and social conditions, which are often seen as a barrier to educational development.

The Six Dimensions of the EFA Targets

- Expansion of early childhood care and developmental activities, including family and community interventions, especially for poor, disadvantaged and disabled children;
- Universal access to, and completion of, primary (or whatever higher level of education is considered as 'basic') by the year 2000;
- Improvement of learning achievement such that an agreed percentage of an age cohort (e.g. 80 per cent of 14 year olds) attains or surpasses a defined level of necessary learning achievement;
- Reduction of the adult illiteracy rate (the appropriate age-group to be determined in each country) to, say, one half its 1990 level by the year 2000, with sufficient emphasis

Contd...

on female literacy of significantly reduce the current disparity between male and female illiteracy rates;

- Expansion of provision of basic education and training in other essential skills required by youth and adults, with programme effectiveness assessed in terms of behavioural change and impact on health, employment and productivity;

- Increased acquisition by individuals and families of the knowledge, skills and values required for better living and sound and sustainable development, made available through all education channels including the mass media, other forms of modern and traditional communication, and social action, with effectiveness assessed in terms of behavioural change.

(Note: The Jomtien Framework for Action invited countries to set their own targets with reference to these dimensions; it was not assumed that all the numerical targets could be met within a decade).

STRENGTHENING THE KNOWLEDGE BASE

During the nineties many countries have improved their capacity to gather and analyse educational data and evaluate performance: preparation of the EFA indicators and the national and regional reports and of the UNESCO World Yearbooks of Education have been a stimulus. National systems are introducing new structures or strengthening existing ones. Examples include the National Qualification Framework in South Africa, the Office for Standards in Education in England and Wales, the system of observatory and evaluation reports in the National Ministry of Education and Culture, France and the expanded evaluation role of the National Institute for Educational Studies and Research, Brazil. By participating in the UNESCO/UNICEF Monitoring Learning Achievements project, more than fifty countries have gained a better understanding of pupils' learning achievements.

4

Achieving the goals: The Six Target Dimensions

What is at issue in the EFA movement is nothing less than a continuing transformation of educational values, structures and procedures in many parts of the world. The focus is education and learning: but changes in social and cultural context, in economic and financial conditions and in the ways communities go about their daily lives are also at issue. For even the most educationally advanced countries, there are profound challenges to meet if the improvements that are sought are to occur in the quality and relevance of what is provided. The goals of universal access and effective, continued learning for all are a constant reminder of unfinished business not only in the poorly resourced and less well managed systems.

The experience of the Jomtien decade has given rise to a multitude of questions and issues as countries and agencies have pursued the targets they set themselves. The way has often not been smooth. There are uncertainties—for example about how to make the most educationally effective use of the new technologies in conditions of scarcity. Partnerships have not always been as comfortable and cooperative as desired—in relations at times between governments and NGOs, or among donor agencies, or between governments and communities.

Differences in belief systems and ideologies and community traditions are to be respected and valued for their diversity and cultural richness. They do not, however, always align well with or provide support for the Jomtien targets. Sometimes they are completely at variance, for example traditions and customary practices regarding the roles of women and girls and their educational needs.

The preference expressed for family rather than institution-based child care raises important issues about community choice and the interaction of universalist values and the particularist preferences of individual cultures and sub-cultures. They are also a constant reminder of scarcity: choices are often forced on families and on children due to unrelenting financial pressure as well as traditional customs. Attainment of the Jomtien targets calls into play a great number of contextual considerations whose variety and impact go a long way towards explaining the continuing, would-wide differences in the attainment of targets.

The numerous educational trends, concerns and issues discussed at Jomtien were, for the purpose of target setting, combined into six Target Dimensions. Countries were invited to set their own course, with reference in some dimensions to quite precise targets. Other targets were much broader and more open. The Framework for Action document was prepared 'as a reference and guide for national governments, international organisations, bi-lateral aid agencies, non-governmental organisations (NGOs), and all those committed to the goal of Education for All in formulating their own plans of action for implementing the World Declaration.' This statement was followed by suggestions for intermediate goal setting, specific time-bound targets and measuring progress. However, these were to be based on a 'realistic appraisal of possibilities'. 'Countries with low literacy and enrolment rates and very limited national resources, will need to make hard choices in establishing national targets within a realistic time frame'. (3) Countries were invited to set their own targets for the 1990s in terms of the six target dimensions. Thus there were two closely related but nevertheless different challenges:

1) to set realistic national and local targets within but not necessarily incorporating all of the Jomtien target dimensions; and 2) to aspire in that target setting to implementation to meet the full range of Jomtien targets and at the level of attainment specified or indicated.

Reporting on progress over the decade has not usually drawn explicitly upon that distinction. But it is extremely important in assessing 'success' or otherwise, to recognise that while all those who adopted the Jomtien Declaration were committed, they were committed to target directions, and not to precisely the same targets in substantive terms. Some of the harsher judgements that have been made do not respect that distinction. On the other hand, the distinction cannot be used as a justification for indifference, misdirection of resources and poor organisation and management.

A combination of sub-national, national, sub-regional and regional reports with statistical underpinning together with specialist studies of cross-cutting themes have been undertaken. These six target dimensions need to be examined from the several perspectives adopted in these reports. Data on trends are not always consistent, nor do they permit reliable comparisons over time or within countries and parts of countries. In many instances, the data that have been assembled are still provisional and subject to correction. With due allowance for these considerations, the data do permit snapshots, for example the achievement of literacy targets in a single district, urban/rural disparities in access to primary schools, or learning achievements across a range of countries. Again, a major theme may be illuminated by a specialist's report on an area where there may be wide disparities across countries but a major interest in all. The new information and communication technologies and the supply and utilisation of educational materials are obvious examples.

Mapping exercises undertaken in the Asia-Pacific region graphically illustrate educational opportunities at specific points of time. For example, geographic and gender inequalities are shown in maps of primary school net enrolment ratios in Nepal, in 1996. These clarify the issues of the markedly lower net enrolment of girls as against boys in many societies, and the lower enrolment of both in rural as against more urbanised areas.

Overall trend analysis based on statistical returns forms part of the accompanying **Statistical Document** and these trends are identified in general statements in the following discussion. However, there are as well numerous specific developments of considerable importance in building up a comprehensive picture of what countries and organisations have achieved in the quest of education for all. A number of these have been selected for illustrative purposes. In a short synthesis summarising overall achievements it is clearly impossible to do justice to the numerous instances of gains—and setbacks—recorded in the country reports and regional syntheses, and reference would need to be made to them for the full details, and of course to the **Statistical Document.**

It is also necessary to keep in mind the overarching themes of Jomtien as discussed in the previous chapter, which cut across all six of the target areas: the very low or variable levels of educational access and opportunity in many countries; the 'lost generation' of adults who had no formal schooling whatsoever, and the need to go beyond attendance requirements and participation rates to the quality and the value to the individual and to society of the learning experience. There is a definite need for new ideas and strategies to bring education from the periphery to the centre of people's lives and of political and social action programmes. Many of the plans and programmes for educational development and reform that countries have adopted during the 90s draw together several of the Jomtien target areas and interrelate a number of the overarching themes.

Extensive bodies of both quantitative and qualitative data have been gathered and analysed for all six target areas. There are three of them—early childhood care and education, participation in primary education and adult literacy—where the information

PRIMARY SCHOOL NET ENROLMENT RATIOS
NEPAL, FEMALE AND MALE, 1996

A snapshot: Enrolment Data on Nepal 1996 to illustrate geographic and gender differences

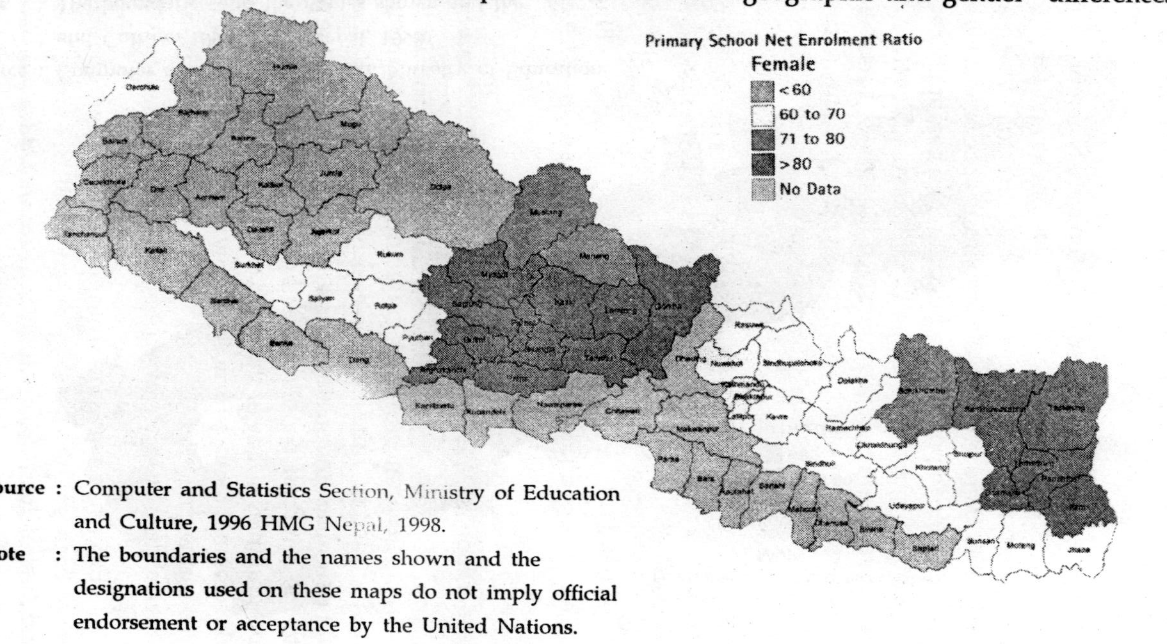

Source : Computer and Statistics Section, Ministry of Education and Culture, 1996 HMG Nepal, 1998.

Note : The boundaries and the names shown and the designations used on these maps do not imply official endorsement or acceptance by the United Nations.

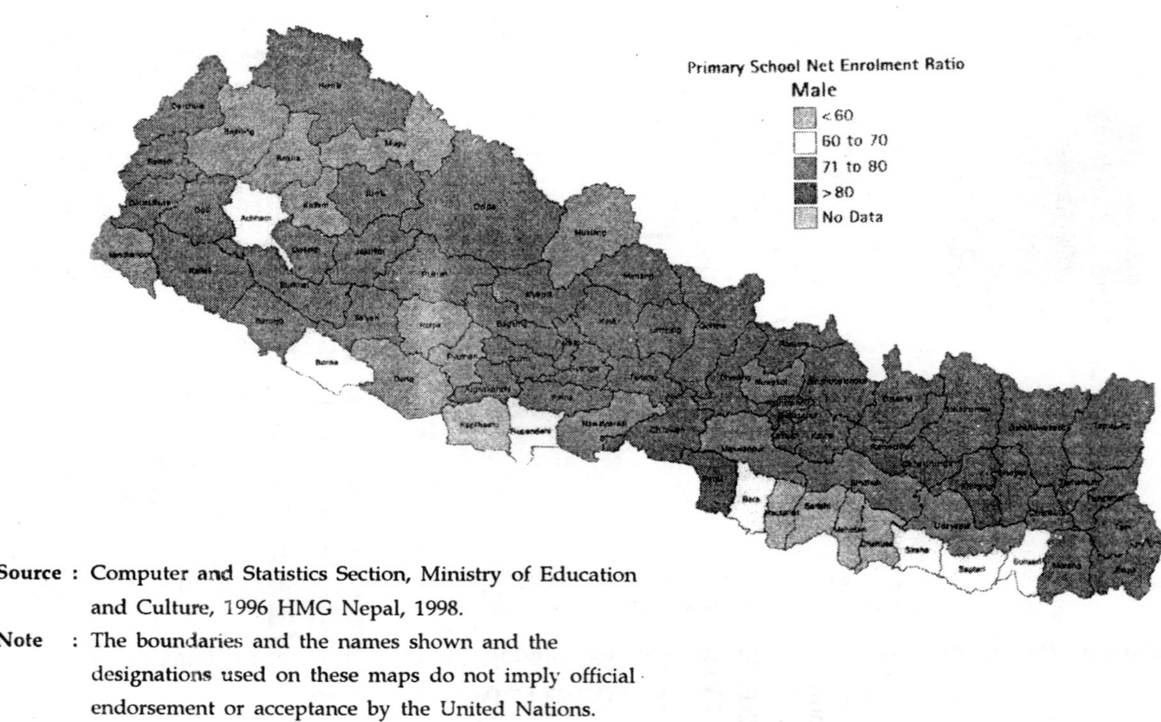

Source : Computer and Statistics Section, Ministry of Education and Culture, 1996 HMG Nepal, 1998.

Note : The boundaries and the names shown and the designations used on these maps do not imply official endorsement or acceptance by the United Nations.

provided in the EFA Assessment is fairly inclusive, if still quite variable. However, there is much less information available on the quality of children's performance in school, youth skills development, and education for a better life. Appraisals of the latter three would require both output data, which are generally either limited or completely lacking, and a considerable amount of values-based judgement. In the EFA 2000 Assessment reports, they are treated discursively, if at all, with comments that are often tentative and very brief. In several reports practically nothing is said about behavioural change, presumably because data are unavailable, or are widely scattered, costly to collect and could not be assembled. In the following section of this Report, the first three target areas named above are treated first and, of necessity, more fully than the latter three.

EXPANSION OF EARLY CHILDHOOD CARE AND DEVELOPMENTAL ACTIVITIES

TARGET DIMENSION: Expansion of early childhood care and developmental activities, including family and community interventions, especially for poor, disadvantaged and disabled children.

The target had two main facets: first the growth of awareness and understanding of the importance of the early years for subsequent development and learning; second, the introduction and extension of structures and programmes to foster and support child development and learning.

The growth of awareness

"The Jomtien Declaration and Framework gave international presence and sanction to early childhood care and development and to 'initial education' in a way that it had not enjoyed previously" (Myers, p.4)

From the available evidence it is a reasonable conclusion that in the Jomtien decade the first aspect – awareness – has been well on the way to being achieved in many countries but by no means all. The main reasons for the success which has been achieved are growing community and professional recognition of the importance of early learning and of the need to reduce risks to health and all-round development.

The second aspect—**implementation**—in some countries had already been achieved at the beginning of the 90s; for others there was notable progress in the course of the decade; for most it is still a goal to be reached. There are also countries where it is not an issue at least not for public policy. But as 'awareness' grows, other things being equal, progress on 'implementation' can be expected, albeit at quite different rates and using quite varied means both private and public.

At the present time, understanding of the vital significance of the early childhood years for development and learning is strongest: in the research community; among policy makers; parents and interest groups in certain countries; some NGOs; and in the major international organisations—those in membership of the EFA Forum, the European Community, Council of Europe and the OECD among others. There is no shortage of policy statements and there are many projects. A small number of countries—France, Belgium, Iceland, New Zealand and Sweden, among them—have well-established, comprehensive programmes reflecting national policy commitments and wide acceptance in the community of the value of a systematic approach. These countries have in place legislation, a regulatory framework, health and welfare provision, appropriate buildings and facilities, curricula and learning resources, well educated personnel, monitoring and evaluation of performance and so on.

Some European countries have perceived the value of consolidated services for children or well developed procedures for co-ordinating public-private provision. In India, a very large intersectoral programme is the Integrated Child Development Service (ICDS).

This programme, for children below the age of six years and pregnant and nursery mothers, is directed at remote areas and for vulnerable children. The need is well recognised and there has been progress but its coverage and outreach are still low.

The very strong provision made over several decades in Eastern and Central Europe deteriorated in the 90s, especially in Eastern Europe. This was due, it seems to a mixture of financial crises, political turbulence and changing views about the role of the state. In these countries there is awareness of the need for and value of well structured programmes, but a limited capacity for the time being to sustain them.

In other countries—Ireland and the United Kingdom, for example—there is official recognition of the value of more structured programmes and the need to extend provision. Procedures are in hand in these countries to develop comprehensive national systems within a strengthened public policy framework, building in some cases on a long history of voluntary care and partial state provision.

In those numerous countries where there is little or no systematic provision of early childhood education and care, where there is only limited formal provision for primary health care and where there are nutritional deficiencies, people may very well understand the need but the capacity to respond is severely constrained. For example, parens often understand the value of health services, good nutrition, creches and nursery classes but lack the means to avail themselves of what may be available. Particularly in rural areas and in the poorest countries, services either do not exist or are so distant as to be effectively unavailable even if they could be afforded.

Overall, however, Jomtien itself and 'the Jomtien decade' have succeeded in placing early childhood education and care, early childhood development and other such formulations on the global agenda, as a necessary foundation for continuing personal, cultural, social and economic development. This can be counted a major achievement which will continue to bear fruit in the years ahead.

Progress in implementation

Enrolments in programmes of early childhood care and education have increased – but these increases are generally small or marginal. There are huge variations across countries, urban areas are more favoured than rural and remote areas and children of better off families have much better opportunities than their peers. However, it is exceedingly difficult to draw firm and detailed conclusions about implementation: the type of provision and its duration vary widely; informal-formal distinctions overlap; private provision is almost certainly under-estimated – and there are widely diverging views about what is to count as high quality provision and outcomes.

Although the general tendency has been for enrolments to increase to a small degree since 1990. Enrolments range from almost zero to 100% across countries. Enrolment tabes based on country returns are given in the thematic study on ECCE, but the author cautions against making comparisons across countries due to the variability of definitions and data and nature of provision.

The introduction and extension of structures and programmes to foster and support child development and learning is the logical next step from awareness of needs and the proclamation of rights. Progress in provision in many countries has been reported, but the facilities and use of human and material resources are highly diversified; no single model emerged as the dominant one in the 90s. Some countries focus on a single pre-school year, others on programmes for 3 to 5/6 year olds, others treat 0 - 5/6 as a continuum of development phases and needs. In accordance with the views of many professionals in the field, South Africa defines early childhood as the first 9 years, thereby bringing the first years of schooling firmly into the 'early childhood' ambit, at least in principle.

States' roles vary from little or no action, to family allowances and parental leave so that children can be kept at home, to subsidised attendance, to fully state financed and run institutions. Several countries in the regions defined by membership of either the European Community or the Organisation for Economic Co-operation and Development, or both, have high levels of provision of various kinds. But participation rates range from very high, through modest to low. In Australia, Canada, Finland, Greece, Ireland, South Korea and Switzerland, for example, participation rates are reported to be less then 25 per cent, whereas in some other (France, Belgium) it is higher than 90 per cent. However there are data difficulties especially in the private sector so such figures need to be treated with considerable caution. For many countries early childhood care and education provision is of lesser priority than, for example, the universalisation of primary schooling or adult literacy campaigns. At least this is so for the formal provision of learning centres, pre-schools and so on.

A distinction must be drawn between primary health care and sound nutrition which are everywhere recognised as essential (though all too commonly not achieved) and formal education provision for pre-school infants and young children which is not universally accepted as necessary or even desirable, at least before 3-4 years of age. Societal changes, however, are leading to more organised provision, including structured learning for children from the earliest years.

Important gains have been made in the scope and direction of health work starting from infancy and extending into the pre-school stage and primary schooling. In several countries, especially those in Sub-Saharan Africa and parts of South Asia, they have been spurred on by the HIV/AIDS disaster. A wide variety of strategies has been deployed to advance disease prevention measures (TB and measles vaccination for example), provide basic hygiene and health training and address nutritional deficiencies. They include cross-ectoral collaboration, parent and community participation, and the development of new tools for assessment of need, planning, monitoring and evaluation. A broader and more interrelated view of health and education has been promoted and analysed through a series of regional and global meetings and reports by the Council of Europe, the Commission of the European Communities, UNICEF, UNDP, USAID and the World Bank. WHO has launched the Global School Health Initiative in support of the health-promoting school which takes the health focus beyond early childhood and into primary and secondary schooling (4).

Most countries have established systems of primary health care for infants and their value is widely acknowledged. Basic health measures and training for adult women have led to large reductions in infant and child mortality. There is evidence of a close, positive relationship between parents' use of health care systems and their valuing of early years' education. Systems of early childhood education can be expected to evolve following improvements in health education of parents and adult literacy programmes.

As already mentioned, the data problem remains acute. No country appears to maintain a system of reporting which adequately encompasses private provision even though in many it is a very large or even major component of ECCE. Although there are some exceptions, most countries have provided little of the information needed for a systematic audit of overall provision in the health, nutritional and psycho-social domains.

The emphasis in EF reporting has been on moves to establish more structured systems of early childhood education but there are so many variations—of definitions, baseline years, length of sessions and duration of programmes that comparative analysis is fraught with difficulty. Much may be happening that is not recorded especially in the conditions affecting provision and performance. For example, in the reports on adult literacy and non-formal education, very little attention has been paid to the uses of literacy in campaigns of parent education, or to the important interaction between parental levels of education and child and infant care and education. Increasingly sophisticated demographic procedures in the 80s and 90s have enable more accurate estimating than hitherto, so figures, however incomplete, are more reliable than in the past.

Of the E9 countries which together contain two thirds of the world's population, only Brazil, China, Mexico and to a lesser degree Indonesia report significant enrolments of pre-school children. In Mexico, almost 80 per cent of 3 to 5 year olds attend pre-school, for one year or more; provision in Brazil is mainly through municipal governments and is particularly important for children whose parents are unschooled; in Indonesia, expansion in coming mainly through the initiatives of NGOs and is often linked with food complements and health services.

Among the gains in E9 countries are strategies tat involve parents and communities and support vulnerable families. In some E9 countries, there has been a substantial increase in pre-school educational services. However, major disparities continue—between urban and rural areas and according to socio-economic levels. Improvements of provision is seen as a major challenge yet is not included in the list of goals adopted in the Declaration of the E-9 Countries made at Recife, Pernambuco, Brazil, February 2000.

The same kind of challenge exists in the Arab countries where the importance of educating 3 to 5 year olds has been increasingly recognised in the 90s, but enrolments remain low-in 8 of 15 countries, it drops to below 10 per cent and in only 2 does it reach 70 per cent. Programmes tend to be limited in duration to one or two years; provision is mainly in private hands; gender disparity still favours boys. In a few countries—Mauritania, Djibouti, Sudan and Yemen—widespread poverty stands in the way of progress; in some, health services are very limited with high rates of infant morality.

GROSS ENROLMENT RATIOS IN EARLY CHILDHOOD DEVELOPMENT

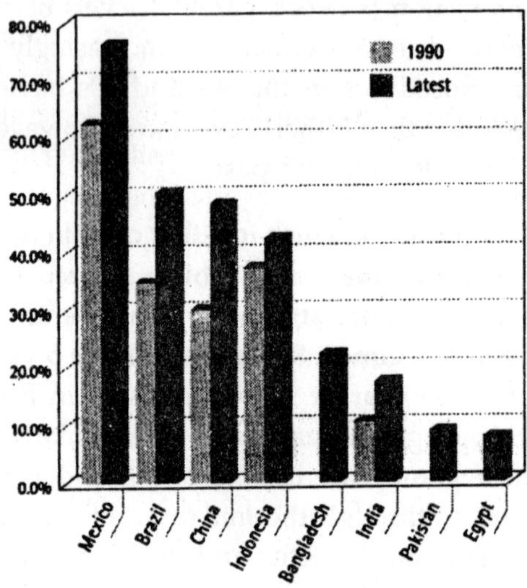

Source : Education for All, the Nine Largest Countries (2000)

A rather different picture emerges in many of the countries of the Asia-Pacific region. Except for Trans-Caucasus and Central Asian countries, where there have been difficulties arising from political, economic and social transformations, rapid growth has occurred. This is most striking in SE Asia sub-region, with a strengthening of professional training and higher education research in the fields of education, health and social welfare. Male-female differences in participation are generally small and many countries report a continuing trajectory of development. There are, in most if not all countries, inequalities affecting children from poorer families and remote areas. With rapid expansion, concerns multiply over narrow curricula, inadequately trained teachers, poor facilities, the lack of a regulatory framework and a weak knowledge base. As in other regions, there is a great variation in the nature of programmes within and between countries. Nevertheless, early childhood care and education has been 'the single most striking element of [the East and South East Asia countries'] development plan'. (5)

There is a notable role for NGOs and private providers in most countries—in the Asia-Pacific region, the Caribbean, Latin America, Africa, Europe and North America. Much is being achieved through their efforts and their continuing role is indispensable in order to make further much needed gains. Yet by committing themselves to the Jomtien Declaration, countries accepted a major public policy responsibility. This takes several different forms: legislation; regulations; negotiation; parental support; subsidies to private providers and the direct operation of creches, nursery classes, pre-schools and so on. A strong, flexible policy framework can incorporate a multiplicity of types of provision and providers.

Several African countries-Zimbabwe, Tanzania and South Africa-are strengthening the public policy role, by such means as developing teacher training curricula, attaching reception classes to primary schools and seeking closer co-operation among separate ministries. Others are treating public policy as a framework for fostering local initiative. However, a large number of countries have yet to move far.

Extremes in African enrolment figures range from the Seychelles and Mauritius (virtually 100 per cent), to 2 per cent or less in countries suffering the ravages of war and economic collapse. Urban-rural differences of opportunity are often extreme and are generally more important than gender imbalance. This is true of most if not all regions. Countries often have difficulty in monitoring and regulating a very diverse provision by a multiplicity of agencies. These might include creches, maternity classes, day nurseries, village day care centres, social centres, orphanages, informal self-help groups, open air centres. A significant emerging initiative is the more intense use of existing community resources, and traditional frameworks which in some countries might include religious schools, child and maternal protection centres and the family circle. In Cuba, a national home and community-based programme aims eventually to reach all children aged 0-6.

In most countries great efforts of quite diverse kinds will be required over the next decade and even further into the future if there is to be a substantial improvement in enrolments and quality of provision. These will involve a multiplicity of agencies, private as well as public. Large numbers of new centres and trained personnel will be required. Building on a decade of solid but still insufficient achievement, Senegal, for example, has estimated that to meet its enrolment targets, provision will have to be made for 278,000 additional young children by 2008, 308 centres and preschool units will have to be constructed and equipped each ear. Major urban rural disparities would need to be overcome and improvements made in the educational programme including health and nutrition, teacher competence, materials and equipment. The scale of operation and requirements would fairly represent the challenge many countries will face; for some there would be much more to accomplish. For all countries which at present make only limited provision there will be difficult priority issues to face, notably as between extending pre-school provision and primary schooling. It is important to achieve greater clarity of purpose and cohesiveness of cross-sectoral responsibilities.

The Jomtien target for ECCE was open-ended in respect of growth, but made explicit reference to the most needy groups. Important gains have been made in many countries, but there are few if any in others. Rural communities seem to be particularly disadvantaged in most countries, worldwide, in terms of provision and access.

UNIVERSAL ACCESS TO AND COMPLETION OF 'BASIC' EDUCATION

TARGET: Universal access to and completion of primary (or whatever higher level of education is considered 'basic') by the year 2000.

Recognising the importance of basic education and of universal primary schooling

For most regions, universal primary schooling is the key target. 'Access to primary education constitutes the greatest concern in all countries', directed at the French, Portuguese and Spanish speaking countries of Africa, this sentiment is shared in the many countries, world-wide, that have yet to meet the Jomtien access and enrolment target and in others. It applies to all countries where access has not been followed by sustained progression rates or a high standard of student performance.

Economic prosperity and social progress depend upon educational reform. This includes extending participation in schooling, broadening the skills base, extending the scope of civic responsibility, building the capacity for responsible civic participation and meeting basic conditions for equity and social justice. Universal participation in primary education over several years' duration and of good quality is proclaimed and accepted in all of the EFA 2000 Assessments as a necessary condition if countries' social and economic goals are to be achieved and individual human rights recognised. Progress—sometimes quite spectacular—is reported in enrolments in primary education across most regions. But there are too many countries and regions within countries where either there has been little or no progress in the decade or actual decline. Major deficiencies continue in Sub-Saharan Africa, South Asia and in some parts of South America. Everywhere there are continuing inequalities within countries. So, while the target may be universally 'recognised', it is not being universally acted on with sufficient seriousness of purpose or being achieved.

There are countries, however, with different concerns. These in the main are the economically advanced countries, where the goal of universal access and completion of primary education has long since been achieved and there are in place highly developed systems of primary, secondary and tertiary education. Yet there are unfulfilled targets, qualitative as well as quantitative at all levels, including primary and pre-school. Quality is the major concern, and this is leading to new and revised standards for student performance; but there are also grounds for concern in the incidence of non-attendance, school violence, poor motivation and changes in family and community life that militate against effective learning. Japan, a country which has had remarkable success in achieving primary and universal secondary education, a national system of kindergartens and day nurseries and highly favourable staff-student ratios, is not alone in reporting problems of school resistance, bullying, drug addiction and over-reliance on highly competitive examinations and selection procedures. Nationwide parent, teacher and student demonstrations in France testify to mounting anxiety over violence at school. School failure and attrition rates in secondary education, including very high rates among specific ethnic and socio-economic groups, and low levels of student motivation are of growing concern in many European countries, North America and Australasia.

What, then, is meant by 'universal'? Enrolment targets for perhaps 100 per cent in relatively prosperous parts of countries are sometimes accompanied by targets of, say, 90 per cent or 95 per cent for poorer, more remote areas. In percentage terms the difference is small, but for large population countries, actual numbers are high. In some countries, completion of a 2-3 year programme is seen as a target for poorer, remote rural areas whereas for cities and the more prosperous areas it may be anything from 4 to 9 years. In countries with long-established systems of primary and secondary education, when dropout and irregular school attendance occur along with poor learning outcomes, there is less than 'universal' completion(6). Social expectations and policy targets in many countries are completion, not just of lower secondary but of upper secondary and/or vocational training and apprenticeship as well.

The reasons from non-completion of full programmes vary and may be very practical. But in these and other ways, widespread abridgements are occurring in practice to targets of 'universal access and completion.'

It is not only the most economically advanced countries that had achieved virtual universal enrolment in primary education by the beginning of the nineties or did so in the course of the

RATIO OF UPPER SECONDARY GRADUATES TO POPULATION AT TYPICAL AGE OF GRADUATION BY TYPE OF PROGRAMME (FIRST EDUCATIONAL PROGRAMME) 1996

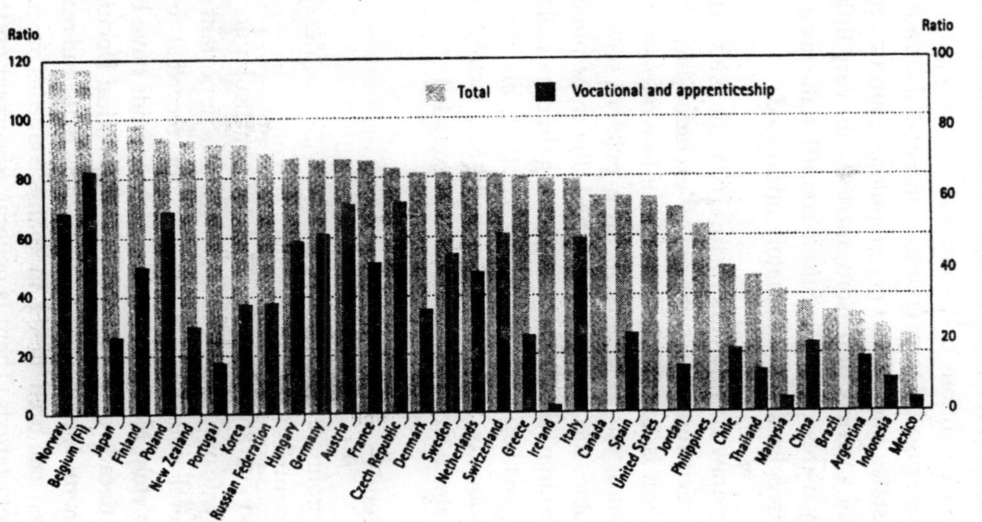

Source : Education at a Glance (1998).

decade. Countries of Eastern and Central Europe, the Trans-Caucasus, and in the Caribbean, several countries of Central and South America and Asia have by the year 2000 reached or have within sight the target of universal or near universal participation in primary and at least lower secondary education. Declines have occurred, however, in some countries due in the main to worsening economic conditions or violent disorder as regimes toppled and civil war spread. Many countries in Sub-Saharan Africa, several Asian states and some very populous countries in South Asia have, for a variety of reasons, made either very little progress or actually regressed. In all of these countries, the need is not always recognised let alone adequately addressed.

To draw attention to structural conditions affecting enrolment and participation, the concepts of 'excluded-included' are being used (7). It is not simply a matter of low rates of enrolment and attendance, but of exclusion, in a positive sense, of the most vulnerable, the most impoverished, the most remotely located, girls, children with disabilities, working children, children suffering the impact of HIV/AIDS. By contrast an inclusive policy, internationally, nationally, regionally and locally, would, by all deliberate means, reach out to the excluded.

The Trends

Enrolment data must be treated with considerable caution—some countries have not reported, and others have qualified their returns in various ways. Trend data in particular are very uneven and private provision, whose growth is an important development in several countries, is usually not recorded or only very incompletely. Nevertheless, the global trends have been mapped for the decade and analysed in the Statistical Document and the thematic study on demographic challenges (8) and real, substantial progress has been made in many countries in achieving the enrolment targets. There is general agreement on the conditions affection trends and on matters for which concentrated attention will be required in the years ahead.

TRENDS IN NET ENROLMENT RATIOS (NER) BY REGION, 1990 AND 1998

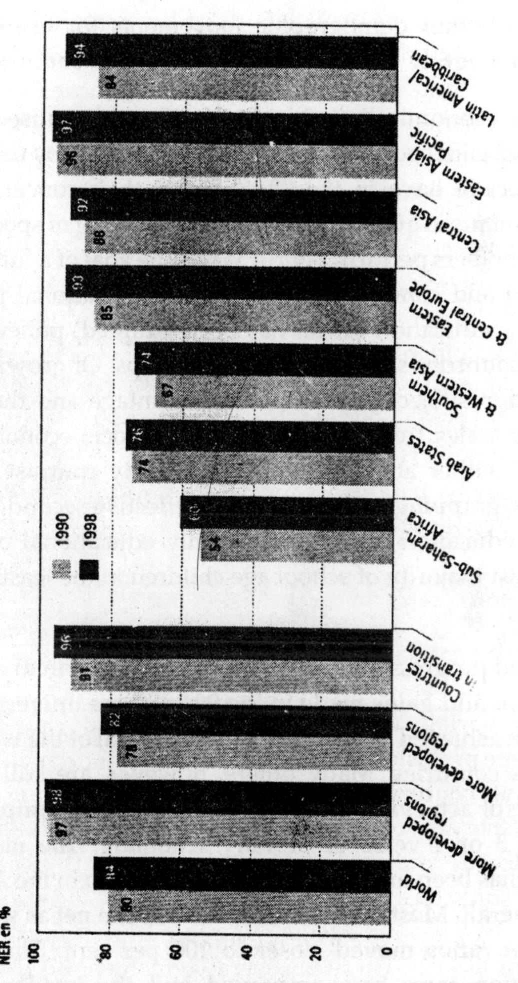

Source : EFA Statistical Document, (2000).

Several countries report either continuing universal participation or major gains. Trends in net enrolment ratios show good gains in most regions and slight gains in others. However they mask considerable variations between and within countries. Also enrolment is not the same as attendance and completion which are highly variable. Enrolment trends must also be seen in light of other demographic movements for example in the number of out of school children in the E-9 countries.

The economically advanced and industrialised countries which had achieved universal primary education by the beginning of the decade have in the 90s directed their concerns towards improvements in quality, including the targeting of specific groups whose members perform poorly. When the goal of a full secondary education and some form of post-school vocational preparation or tertiary education for all has been adopted, policy initiatives in these countries single out 'at risk' groups. Of growing concern are children subject to multiple disadvantage and the incidence of young males from certain ethnic and socio-economic groups who are neither at school nor in work. By contrast with these countries, grapping with problems of effective secondary schools, primary education represents the only educational opportunity for the vast majority of school age children in the least developed countries.

Good progress, reflecting a decline in the primary school age population and gains made in the 90s will see universal primary education achieved by the year 2010 in several of the world's most populous countries. Many others, however, are still facing the challenge of achieving universal enrolment and completion of as much as 3 or 4 years of primary schooling. The most notable progress has been in East Asia and Oceania and in the Asia-Pacific region overall. Most of these countries have in net as well as gross enrolment ratios moved closer to 100 per cent. That is to say, participation rates have improved and the incidence of age-appropriate enrolments has increased, reflecting greater internal efficiencies. South Asian enrolment increases, however, have barely kept up with the growth rate in the population of school-age children, due both to high fertility and survival rates reflecting improved health care and nutrition. In the East and Southeast Asian sub-region, gender disparity has decreased. It remains marked, though, in some countries in South and West Asia, especially in remote and rural provinces of a few countries. These disparities reflect rapid population growth and the absence of wide-ranging structural reforms. Completion rates have improved in some but not all countries. Out-of-school numbers also remain high, underlining the problem in many countries of continuing population increases.

Modest, steady progress in the countries of the Caribbean and South and Central America has resulted in a decline in the number of children out of school. Similar progress has occurred for children in school in the Arab States and some parts of Sub-Saharan Africa (but the overall number of children out-of-school in these regions has increased). While enrolment increases are generally either matching or exceeding the population growth rate, it is still a struggle to reduce the out-of-school population. In Sub-Saharan Africa, where there is a disproportionate balance of least developed countries, continuing high population growth rates in combination with other factors make it extremely difficult for many countries to bring about significant reductions in the number of out-of-school children.

The positive global trends mask great contrasts between countries and serious internal disparities A number of factors which are militating against achievement of the Jomtien target temper the optimism that the gross figures generate.

The major world region experiencing the greatest difficulty in the making progress, and in some respects has actually regressed, is Sub-Saharan Africa. The dire plight of children who are the casualties of war in several of these countries has been the subject of worldwide publicity. Not so well publicized are the trends which indicate nothing short of a major crisis in the context

TRENDS IN NUMBERS OF SCHOOL-AGE CHILDREN IN AND OUT OF SCHOOL, 1990 AND 1998

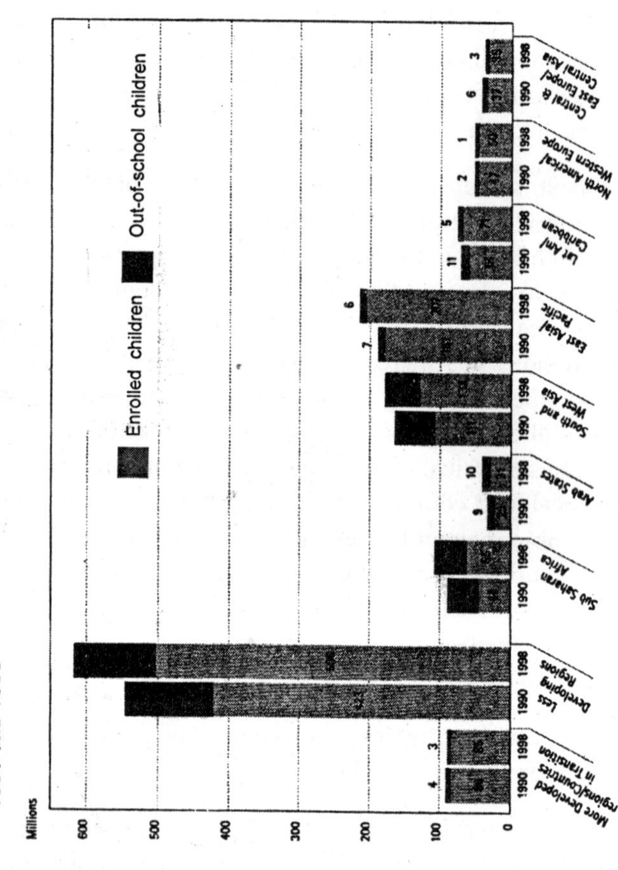

Source : EFA Statistical Document, (2000).

of Education for All. One third of the population of Sub-Saharan Africa was reported in 1999 by FAO to be undernourished. In countries that have experienced long wars, vast numbers of people are displaced. In the tropical zone, which covers a large area of Sub-Saharan Africa, life expectancy is much lower than in the temperate zone, a function of the interaction of disease and poverty-and short life expectancy is a powerful cause of impoverishment (as well as resulting from it). The bottom ten on the UNDP Human Development Index are all Sub-Saharan African countries. The HIV/AIDS pandemic in this region, according to UNAIDS figures, far exceeds that of any other region. Population is increasing at a faster rate than any other region and there are increasing problems of overcrowding in cities and towns. The quality of education, health and other services has declined. Over 40 million primary school age children are not in school; there are very large disparities-gender, urban-rural and others and great contrasts between countries.

Yet, in the face of these critical conditions, while most Sub-Saharan African countries have fallen far short of the primary education target (and all the others), and some participation rates have worsened, a few countries have managed to perform well. They include Botswana, Cape Verde, Malawi, Mauritius, and South Africa where primary enrolment rates are 90 per cent or more. Some countries that started with low enrolment figures have significantly improved over the decade—Malawi, Mozambique and Uganda—others have stabilised high rates—Mauritius, and Seychelles. Some countries have lost ground—Kenya and Zimbabwe, among them; others have remained with very low figures, Liberia and Sierra Leone included.

This is not, of course, the whole picture and many different factors have to be taken into account in explaining lack of progress of decline. But a key point is that countries can succeed, with commitment, strategic planning based on realistic goals and leadership, good management and competent personnel. Despite the tremendous difficulties these have been shown to be attainable.

Economic and social conditions

Economic conditions, ranging from stagnation to inflation to collapse, are widely identified as the major constraint on the supply of schools and teachers, teaching-learning materials and structures for monitoring and evaluating progress and pinpointing areas of difficulty. They affect all levels and forms of education but their impact falls unequally, exacerbating problems of provision and access in rural areas, for poorer families and, in some countries, the opportunities for girls and women.

'Debt remains a major constraint on Caribbean countries in sustaining previous investments in education and in making new ones' (9). The combination of increasing public debt in some countries and declining disposable income in certain sectors of the population, inhibits the needed mix of public and private financing to drive forward the Jomtien agenda on enrolment and participation.

Yet the level of a country's wealth is not always the determinant of school performance. Countries vary considerably in their levels of investment in education and in the vigour and efficiency with which education targets are pursued. By contrast with countries where there are static or declining levels of investment, major funded reform initiatives have been taken, for example in Brazil, where there have been increases in teacher salaries, a more equitable distribution of funds and a concentration of effort in areas of greatest need. The importance of sound financial management has not featured in all the EFA 2000 Assessment reports but is emphasised in the South and East Africa synthesis and in the thematic study by Ablett and Slengesol on the East Asian Financial shock. It is a subject which should be receiving more attention, as a condition of successful implementation of programmes.

In the Sub-Saharan region, while in several countries there has been positive per capita economic growth and more robust economic policies are in place, some economies are devastated by civil war, and others suffer the burdens of social unrest or large scale involuntary population movements including refugees from war zones. The HIV/AIDS pandemic is a human and social tragedy, and also an economic threat. There is overdependence on development assistance to meet basic needs, domestic debt has risen rapidly in some countries, there are large numbers of unemployed youth and adults especially in urban centres and many are inadequately prepared for changing labour markets. Such conditions stand in the way of the increased investment needed to boost primary school enrolments, strengthen retention rates and bring about the needed qualitative improvements. At the same time, they do not provide the right signals for improving efficiency and introducing more innovative ways of using existing resources.

There are many conditions affecting countries' achievement of targets for enrolment and participation. The quality of leadership and the mobilisation of the population have been conspicuous in several African countries (but absent in others) and in China and Brazil among the countries where large gains have been made. The drive to achieve universal enrolment in basic schooling whether at the primary or secondary stage, usually means a struggle with the last 15 or 20 per cent composed of cultural, religious and linguistic minorities, remote populations, nomads, pastoralists and migratory agricultural workers, the severely handicapped, street children and some others. Adolescents in economically advanced countries, particularly for some ethnic groups and in poorer parts of cities, have shown great resistance to schooling, creating another potential '15-20 per cent problem. Mass education means among other things that there is no longer the economic and social status of the former selective systems.

Population increase and movements

Increasing enrolment figures are a function of population increases as much as they reflect an improved capacity to increase participation rates. Africa, for example, continues its upward population trajectory, as does South Asia (but at a lower rate), while other countries have achieved either a significant slowdown in the rate of increase or a stable population. Rapid population growth, combined with weak economic condition, is a major impediment to increased participation and a better quality of schooling. As the Gross Enrolment Rate tables (GER) demonstrate, increased enrolments are not always a source of satisfaction. They may reflect such departures from norms as repeating the grade and overage participation.

Enrolments have also been affected by both voluntary and enforced migration—declines in some areas resulting from the devastating effects of natural disaster, war and civil unrest—and increases in others where refugees are concentrated with resulting pressures on what are often already over-stretched and inadequate facilities. Cities and towns in many countries are becoming over-crowded as population rates soar and rural emigration increases. There are both positive and negative effects of the flight to cities—services, for example, are more readily provided in urban than remote rural areas. On the other hand, very rapid urban growth rates, accompanied by unemployment and poverty, linguistic and cultural differences, are a great strain on existing services designed for much smaller numbers in more stable conditions.

Natural disaster, warfare and civil disturbances

Some countries, prone to cataclysmic events—regular hurricanes and cyclones, large scale flooding, volcanoes, or earthquakes—are under much greater pressure than those where conditions are more or less equable. It has been suggested that climatic changes over recent decades are increasing the incidence of several of these phenomena. Massive floods in Bangladesh and Mozambique and volcanic activity, drought and hurricanes in others not only cause immediate damage and loss of life, but interrupt schooling in countries that may already be under acute pressure to meet growing demand for basic services including primary education. The scale of the refugee problem is an indicator of disruption. Peaking at the all time high of 18 million if 1992, it declined by 1998—but still to a figure of 11.5 million (10).

The scale of warfare and violence in several countries during the 90s is a bitter blow to the hopes and aspirations at the end of the 80s. A combination, then, of large scale political changes in Central and Eastern Europe, democratisation, and improved economic conditions, especially in parts of Asia, seemed to herald a more peaceful and prosperous decade ahead. However, the all-too familiar patterns of civil war and coups together with changing economic fortunes, especially in countries whose economic depend heavily on commodity export, has led to stagnation in rates of primary school participation or real decline.

As stated in the regional synthesis report on South and East Africa, 'Restoration of peace and economic growth are essential for the children to be able to go back to school and normal life'. For planning purposes, educational services need to be differentiated—in different parts of countries and for various stages of conflict, from the battlefield itself to the rehabilitation of traumatised children and child soldiers. But not all countries challenged by war appear to have experienced significant declines in enrolment—Rwanda for example.

A very interesting response to what appears to be a growing incidence of disaster and crises in some of the poorest parts of the world is reported in the thematic study on **Education in Situations of Emergency and Crisis.** Educational crisis strategies are being developed and implemented to re-establish basic education services, reducing the traumatic effects and enabling early return to normality wherever conditions allow this. The Machel Report on the **Impact of Armed Conflict on Children** has heightened awareness of the issue and of the need for the rapid provision of emergency education services. The UNICEF report, **Education in Emergencies and For Reconstruction,** states 'Any emergency education programme must be a development programme and not merely a stop-gap measure that will halt when a particular situation is no longer experiencing intense media coverage' (11).

Is there a need for new structures and modalities?

The roots of the primary school are buried deep in history. It is not just a western invention, but draws its strength and character in part from the great Oriental religions and long established practices for the initiation of children into the social and economic life of traditional societies. Its long and mostly successful history in achieving literate populations and solid bases for continuing learning in many countries helps to explain the continuing worldwide importance and prestige of the primary school. Colonisation, trade and missionary activities have contributed to its place and standing as the key instrumentality of formal learning throughout Africa, Asia, the Pacific, the Americas and Europe.

But the demonstrated inability of a number of countries, some very large, to meet or move strongly towards the target of universal access and participation has led some observers to question whether formal schooling is indeed the way ahead. For them, the school may not be the means to further progress in achieving universal education. This point of view derives not only from inability to meet enrolment targets, but from high rates of dropout and non-completion, poor performance and dysfunctional over-age enrolments. The use of primary schools for over-age students has been necessary, but is increasingly seen to be inappropriate. Interest in non-formal models complementary to primary schools is noted in some countries (Mali, Guinea and Senegal), and reflects the need to provide basic education for children and particularly women who do not find primary schools suitable for their needs or for whom there are no available schools.

It is quite excessive to claim that the formal institution of the primary school as such stands in the way of achieving universal basic education. Yet it is becoming increasingly clear that a variety of means in addition to the conventional pattern of primary schooling is needed in order to attain the Jomtien targets in some countries and regions. Countries are mobilising additional resources, such as the Q'ranic schools in Nigeria, which have been effective in lowering illiteracy rates.

Although distance education, including the use of telematics and broadcasting has not been shown as the answer to providing expanded opportunities for the primary school age group, their value as ancillaries and for secondary teaching and adult education has been demonstrated. Also, they can be of great value in situations of chronic instability or where educational systems are being rebuilt. Further developments, including cost reduction and a readiness to change some of the formalities and the rigidities of the schooling model, should see a wider use of multimedia and new delivery systems for primary age children. Overall the primary school, however modified and extended, seems set to remain the essential instrument for universal education of younger children and, in many countries, adolescents.

THE GENDER QUESTION

Continuing low participation rates for girls in whole countries and parts of countries (rural areas) and social sectors (low socio-economic) continued through the decade. They constitute major hurdles to reaching Jomtien targets. In some countries, of growing importance is the low performance of boys—school alienation and dropout, such that although enrolment targets in primary schools are met, those for retention and progress in learning are not. This problem is referred to, for example, in the reports on Brazil and the Caribbean region. Boys' continuation (and performance) throughout secondary schooling is now high on the agenda of industrialised countries in Europe, North America and in Australia and New Zealand. For this reason, some reports draw attention to the need in future to give a new emphasis to the relevance and quality of school as a means of motivating boys to perform well and continue in schools.

It is, however, the rate of girls' participation in primary schooling that remains a major obstacle, particularly in rural areas. The marked regional variation in school attendance of 8 year old

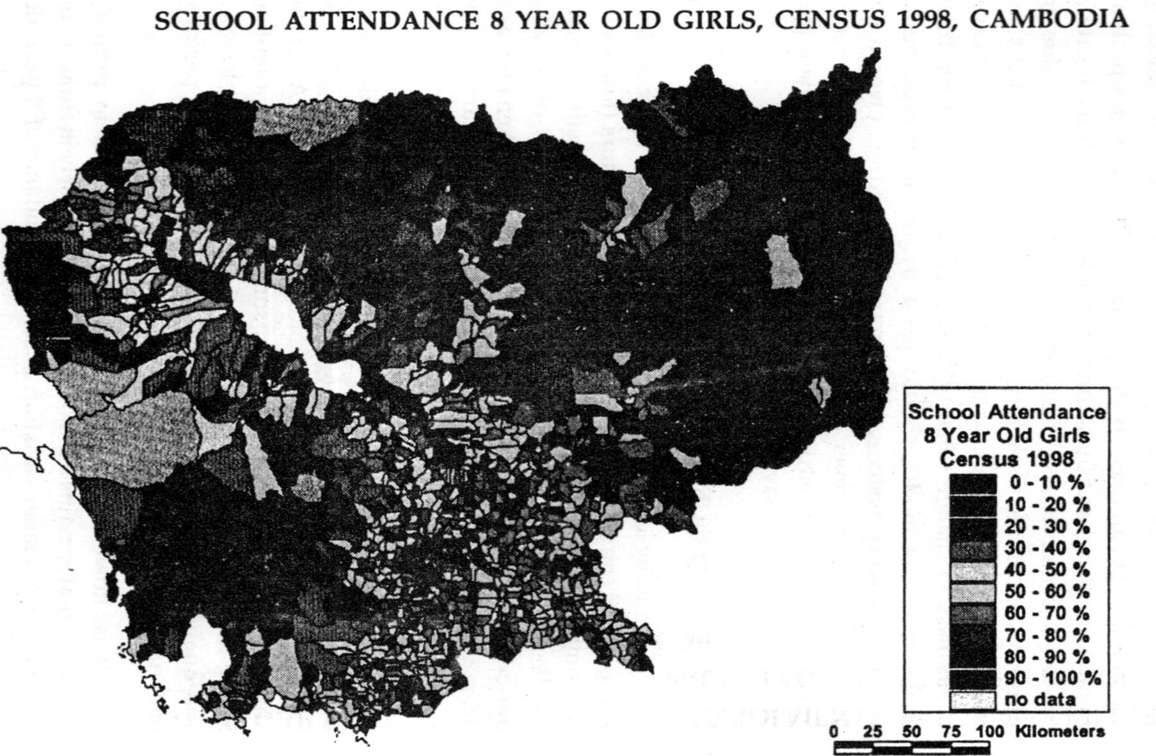
SCHOOL ATTENDANCE 8 YEAR OLD GIRLS, CENSUS 1998, CAMBODIA
School Attendance
8 Year Old Girls
Census 1998
0 - 10 %
10 - 20 %
20 - 30 %
30 - 40 %
40 - 50 %
50 - 60 %
60 - 70 %
70 - 80 %
80 - 90 %
90 - 100 %
no data
0 25 50 75 100 Kilometers

GENDER GAP (M-F) IN ESTIMATED NET ENROLMENT RATIOS OF PRIMARY SCHOOL AGE, 1990-1998 (SHOWING PERCENTAGE POINTS DIFFERENCES BETWEEN MALE AND FEMALE NET ENROLMENT RATIOS)

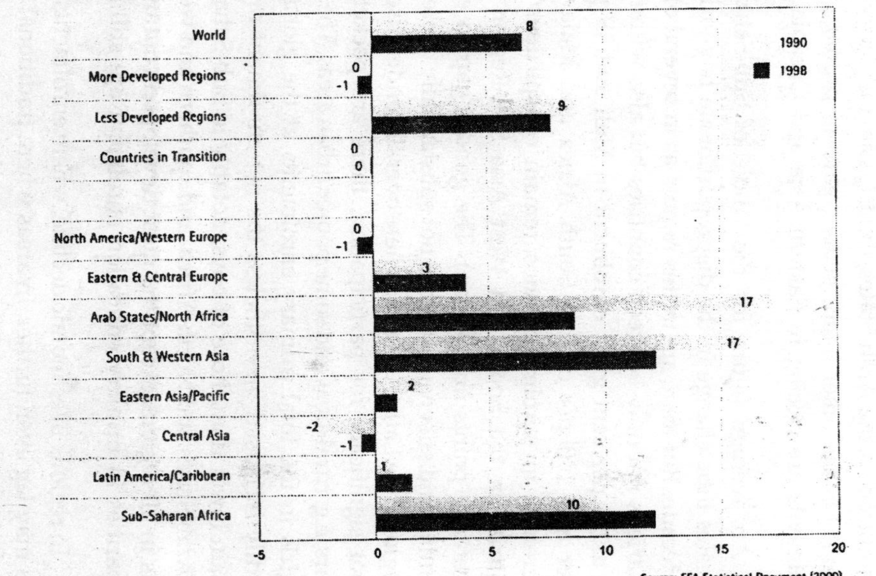

Source : EFA Statistical Document, (2000).

girls within Cambodia for 1998, illustrates the problem. The areas of low school attendance broadly parallel areas of low population density and low adult female literacy rates.

The gender gap has narrowed globally, but there remain considerable regional variations, and disparities are still particularly pronounced in the Arab States, South Asia and the Sub-Saharan regions. On the other hand, gender gaps in primary school age enrolments are closing in Eastern Asia and Oceania.

An average figure for the whole of Sub-Saharan Africa indicates little change in the disproportionate boy-girl ratio over the decade. But there are in this region, as in several others, huge disparities not only between countries but also within them—as low as 16 per cent girls' enrolment in Mali and 19 per cent in Niger and 100 per cent in South Africa and Malawi. Gender differences in enrolment ratios remain conspicuous in several countries in the South and West Asia Sub-Region (above 30 percentage points in Pakistan). The gender gap in enrolments, retention and survival rates has not substantially decreased. Even in regions like Latin America, where overall gender discrimination is not significant for participation, there are pockets where it occurs, e.g. rural areas and some poorer urban areas. The proportion of girls in the total primary enrolments at the global level has steadily increased; nevertheless the net enrolment rates of girls remain lower than those of boys, notably in Sub-Saharan Africa, the Arab States and North Africa, and southern and western Asia. Thus in all regions except the most developed countries, gender disparities in primary education enrolment are still large.

In regions in economic decline, where enrolments are falling, girls may lag even further. In areas where traditional beliefs and practices remain strong, girls may be expected to become homekeepers, child minders and wives at an early age; there are also taboos regarding the education of girls in male-dominated schools, and a lack of gender-friendly curricula and school culture. Counter trends are, however, emerging in some countries—for example in Lesotho where boys are under-represented because they find jobs in nearby South African mines where literacy and education qualifications are not required. But what happens as mines close? Young males then will have neither jobs nor education.

The gender factor interacts with that of regional differences and income levels: girls in poorer rural and isolated areas tend to be under-represented in schools even though, when they are present, they are tending to perform better, for example in literacy and in the lower grades as represented in the Monitoring Learning Achievement study in Africa, and in a slight overall superiority in Kazakhstan and a greater superiority in some Arab countries.

The Environment of the School

It is generally in countries with advanced economies, well developed and stable political and social structures, strong legislation, consistent, long-standing inclusive policies, a well educated teaching force and a highly developed capacity to organise, administer and monitor school systems that primary education has become universal and gained in quality. Even so there are cracks in the edifice which are causing great concern.

Notably in depressed urban areas increased levels of bad behaviour and school violence are reported, for example in the USA, Japan and several European countries. Not only in the relatively depressed areas, teachers are experiencing difficulties in maintaining high levels of children's commitment to learning. Multiple deprivation especially in poorer areas of cities has depressed student attainment levels and aggravated absenteeism. Some countries have initiated special programmes with additional support focused on the most depressed areas: the French ZEPs (Educational Priority Zones) are one of several examples of this concentration of resources. While accurate figures on truancy, low performance and dropout are not available, some estimates suggest that perhaps as much as one tenth to one fifth (or more) of the school age population in some areas, while enrolled, is not effectively participating. In some countries the proportion not completing a full secondary (and hence 'basic') education is considerably higher. A related phenomenon which is equally disturbing is that a high proportion of students completing secondary education do not in fact acquire formal qualifications of value either in the labour market or for further study. They appear in the enrolment statistics, including those for net enrolments, but what the students are actually learning is often of very limited value.

It is not simply access and participation rates that matter. One of the historical reasons for establishing the universal primary and then secondary school was to ensure stability and civic order in emerging democracies. The reform of primary and secondary education has as one of its motives the avoidance of social disintegration in conditions of rapid economic and social change. A major concern at the end of the 20th century in large urban centres and ethnically mixed societies is fostering tolerance and harmony amongst quite diverse groups. It is therefore through the interactions of the two targets—universal participation and the quality of learning processes and outcomes-that the Jomtien agenda is being pursued and needs to be taken further. Success in one is insufficient without the other.

The achievements is relation to the quality target are taken up below. For the participation target there is a mixture of gains and setbacks.

REDUCTION OF THE ADULT ILLITERACY RATE

TARGET: Reduction of the adult illiteracy rate (the appropriate age-groups to be determined by each country), to, say, one half its 1990 level by the year 2000, with sufficient emphasis on female literacy to significantly reduce the current disparity between male and female illiteracy rates.

Changing concepts of literacy

Literacy has over the years been given a variety of interpretations, from the earlier idea of a deficit to be overcome in the basic skills of reading and writing in the mother tongue, to the much broader concept of the making of and active participation in a literate culture, at the individual, local, national and regional levels (12). Terms such as literate environments, a culture of reading, post-literacy, continuing and non-formal education and adult education and adult learners give some indication of the scope and diversity of reporting. Just as measures like levels of government spending on non-formal education and family and community support are used as proxies of commitment to literacy programmes, so 'adult literacy' is itself a proxy for a wide array of adult learning outcomes.

During the 90s, literacy has come to be accepted as a product of a complex interplay of factors: cultural, social-economic and educational, not a disorder or disease that can be swiftly and effectively eradicated (13). The older operational notions of literacy (grade-level, decoding or deciphering competence with written text) were complemented in the 1960s by the broader concept of functional competence in society. This refers to higher level abilities, those enabling people to function in the community and the workplace, to achieve personal goals and develop personal knowledge and potential. This broadening of the concept implies a close attention to contexts, uses, applications and changing relationships between the individual and society. A crucial example is the impact of technology and the consequent need for more people to become technologically literate, that is, capable of making effective use of the instruments for communication and information processing that are becoming available. Visual literacy including the ability to read graphs and diagrams is an issue that arises. Technological literacy is highly advanced in some groups and in some countries, not at all in others. The growing gap between those who are-or can be-technologically literate and those who are not has emerged in the 90s as a theme equal in importance to the longer standing consensus over the need for students to have access to printed texts.

However, all definitions start with the ability to handle printed text. Minimal definitions continue to be used, for example in the compilation of statistics. Even then, some interesting variants occur. For example, the criteria in the Chinese Regulations on Eradicating Literacy are

> 'the recognition of 1,500 Chinese characters for peasant and 2,000 characters for staff and workers in business/enterprises and urban dwellers, the ability of reading simple and easy newspapers and articles, the ability of keeping simple accounts, and the ability of writing simple practical writings.' (14)

UNESCO's definition of the adult literacy rate, as used in the EFA Technical Guidelines to countries, is the percentage of the population aged 15 years and over who can both read and write with understanding a short simple statement on his/her everyday life. But countries were also invited to report on 'literate environments' and learning opportunities especially for women, ethnic and cultural minorities, socially disadvantaged groups and others with special learning needs.

Thus, the first question arising is the nature of the different targets that are being addressed by individual countries and within countries, for different groups. If in many advanced economies, there is universal completion of 8 to 10 years of schooling (and more) and measured reading levels at school are fairly high it might appear that the target of basic literacy has been met. However, recent studies in economically developed countries suggest that between 10 and 20 per cent of the adult population have difficulty with basic reading, writing and numeracy skills.

The approach that takes completion of several years of primary schooling as a proxy for adult literacy is not always satisfactory. For example, countries often express satisfaction if a rate of, say, 80 per cent literacy is reached by a given age-grade level, but may not devote adequate attention to the remaining 20 per cent; also, rapid technological and workplace changes and an increased demand for more diffused civic and social responsibilities mean that skills acquired in primary school are insufficient. Such skills, what is more, have been shown to deteriorate if not well exercised.

Thus there are several aspects of literacy to consider: basic skills acquisition; targets for the low performers; active participation in a literate culture, concepts such as technological and visual literacy; changing contexts for the uses of literacy; and the maintenance and development of literacy once basic skills have been acquired. In adopting the restricted UNESCO definition of basic literacy, countries can report big gains, and several of them do. These are of course of special importance but it must not be forgotten that the figures do not capture the broader concepts of literacy which are of growing significance as illiteracy, worldwide, in its most basic or rudimentary form slowly diminishes.

Literacy trends

Literacy campaigns have a long history, well predating the Jomtien decade. They are part of a constant struggle to create wholly literate societies.

During the 90s there have been real gains even though the number of illiterate people remains very high and in some parts of the world is increasing. There were an estimated 895 million illiterates in the world in 1990, 887 million in 1995, and an estimated 875 million in 2000. The large majority are women, in developing countries.

In Arab countries as a whole, only moderate gains are reported in reducing the overall illiteracy rate; differences between and within countries are great. Gender disparities actually increased in this region, reflecting the continuing cultural bias against enrolling and teaching females. For the region as a whole, there has been an increase in the literacy rate but of only 10 per cent in the decade (from 51.3 per cent to 61.5 per cent). Widespread illiteracy is reported to be the main obstacle to achieving the goals of education for all in the Arab countries at the beginning of the 21st century. In the Arab States' regional report, it is estimated that there are 68 million illiterate people of whom 43 million are female. A quarter of these are found in one country, Egypt (17 million), and 70 per cent in five countries: Egypt, Sudan, Algeria, Morocco and Yemen. Illiteracy in most of these countries is linked with high population density, poverty, and rural areas.

PERCENTAGE OF ADULTS LITERATE IN AFRICA AND MIDDLE FAST

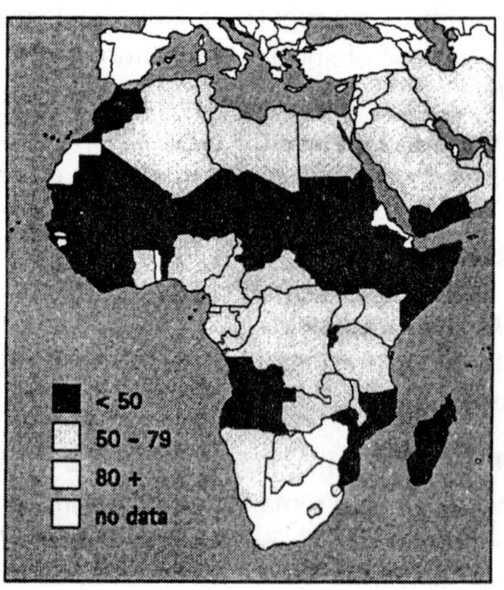

Source : Sub-Saharan Africa Draft Regional Synthesis, Harare Sept-Oct.1999.

Large as these numbers are, they are dwarfed by those from South Asia. In both Bangladesh and India nearly half the adult population are still illiterate and in Pakistan the adult literacy rate is lowest in the subregion at 40 per cent in 1998, with a very low rate of improvement (0.7 per cent) per annum between 1991 and 1998. Sub-Saharan Africa includes a band of countries with 50 per cent or less literacy extending from West Africa through the Sahara to East Africa (where overall illiteracy levels match those of South Asia) and also Angola, Mozambique and Madagascar.

But on the African continent, sometimes in adjacent or nearby countries, adult literacy rates are reported to be as high as 90 per cent (Swaziland) or 77 per cent (Kenya). These figures indicate progress and success or near success in meeting targets. Explanations for these wide variations are not provided in the regional syntheses but certainly bear investigation in future work. High levels of literacy in some African countries support the argument that attainment of the Jomtien goals is possible. With allowance for setbacks that result from major crises, countries can with sufficient determination bring about the improvements that their commitments to the Jomtien Declaration requires.

There have been important gains: and there is a greater realisation by governments, communities and the non-government sector and the international agencies of the need for yet more intensive efforts. Both the continuance of established, effective literacy programmes and the introduction of new ones are required, to achieve significant increases in the number of literates and decreases in the number of illiterates. Some countries—Maldives and Sri Lanka, for example—which have achieved high or near universal basic literacy rates, are taking the path of improved functional literacy, so for them the targets are of a different order than in those countries where basic literacy for all remains a distant goal.

Of particular interest are the sub-national programmes upon which so much depends in heterogeneous countries with very large populations. For example in India, District Level Total Literacy Campaigns (TLCs) have resulted in a rate of literacy about 80 per cent in some districts. This so-called 'campaign mode' at the village level depends on people's participation and low costs, involves NGOs and adopts a variety of strategies. Yet, despite quite dramatic gains in some districts early in the 90s, progress slowed. There are different versions of the facts and the explanation for them, but it seems clear that the focus on community self-help, voluntary action and a policy of saturation could effect major gains (16).

Many NGOs have shown initiative in literacy drives including the targeting of illiteracy among women and girls, for example the activities of the Associations of University Women and other organisations in Africa, South Asia, Latin America and the Pacific region as reported in the assessment by Berewa Jommo *Gender Dimensions in Education for All. NGO and Civil Society Experiences.* Often of a highly local nature, such initiatives where they cannot effect significant advances in the education of girls and women, at least aim to prevent further erosion in the most difficult areas. These interventions underscore the crucial interrelationships between socio-cultural attitudes towards girls and women, occupations and poverty.

Mention is made in several reports of the great difficulty of reaching reliable estimates of literacy rates—the lack of clear indicators and of available and accessible information, the multiple, varied efforts of NGOs and community groups and definitional issues already mentioned. One problem is that adult literacy rates are estimated on the basis of self-proclaimed literacy, during surveys or census taking. This is a very rough and ready mechanism, subject to a high degree of estimating error. Figures, too, are sometimes manipulated: it can be important that programmes are seen to be succeeding even when they are not. In these circumstances it cannot be too emphatically stated that the empirical foundations of figures, percentages, rates of change are very often shaky. They must always be accompanied by the on-the-ground judgements and appraisals by those responsible for and involved in the programmes. In the summaries provided in the regional syntheses, notice is taken of accounts of success—or indeed of misfortune and the explanations for them—as much as it is of overall trends.

Despite the continuing literacy drives, progress is often slow. In Bangladesh, Pakistan and parts of Brazil, both basic literacy and the more broadly defined functional literacy rates continue to be a cause for concern. The Recife Declaration of the E-9 countries thus gives the highest priority to eradication of adult illiteracy.

There are many countries reporting little if any increase in literacy rates—programmes do not match population increases, or are undermined by civil strife, disease, immigration, poor retention rates and other disabling factors. Yet there have been gains in the face of great problems and setbacks in some regions and countries. Eradication of illiteracy is extremely difficult, but it is possible over time and with the necessary commitment and effort.

In many parts of the world, the challenge is to enable adults who have had no formal schooling at all or only the barest minimum to acquire basic skills. But the Jomtien goal is far more ambitious than this: to cut the 1990 illiteracy rate by half. Moreover, the definition of literacy cannot be fixed at the minimum level of operation but has to expand to incorporate increasing expectations of inter-personal and official communications, social and cultural life, and economic activity.

It is doubtful whether the Jomtien target as stated was achieved in the 90s in any of the numerous countries with large numbers of illiterate people. Big differences still remain or have sometimes even increased between urban and rural areas, richer and poorer elements in the population, and minority and majority populations. Females are still discriminated against. This indicates a need to focus campaigns on the most deprived groups and difficult areas, even if a likely consequence is a relatively slow rate of progress in reaching some of them. Blanket targets, setting percentage reductions for the whole country, are likely to be less useful than more precise targeting taking account of key variables-demographic, geographic location, occupational profiles, socio-economic conditions, ethnicity, local traditions and customs, gender ad so on. Figures on illiteracy (age 15+), for example, show huge variations according to 'racial origin'—in Brazil ranging from 5.4 per cent to 50.8 per cent in the 1991 census.

Across much of India adult female literacy rates are either low or very low, as illustrated by the detailed district level data given in the map from the 1991 census. These data have been used to target district level programme funding. For example, UNFPA's current five-year cycle of funding is based on a composite index of mortality, female literacy and fertility (rather than economic indicators)

ADULT LITERACY RATE – FEMALE

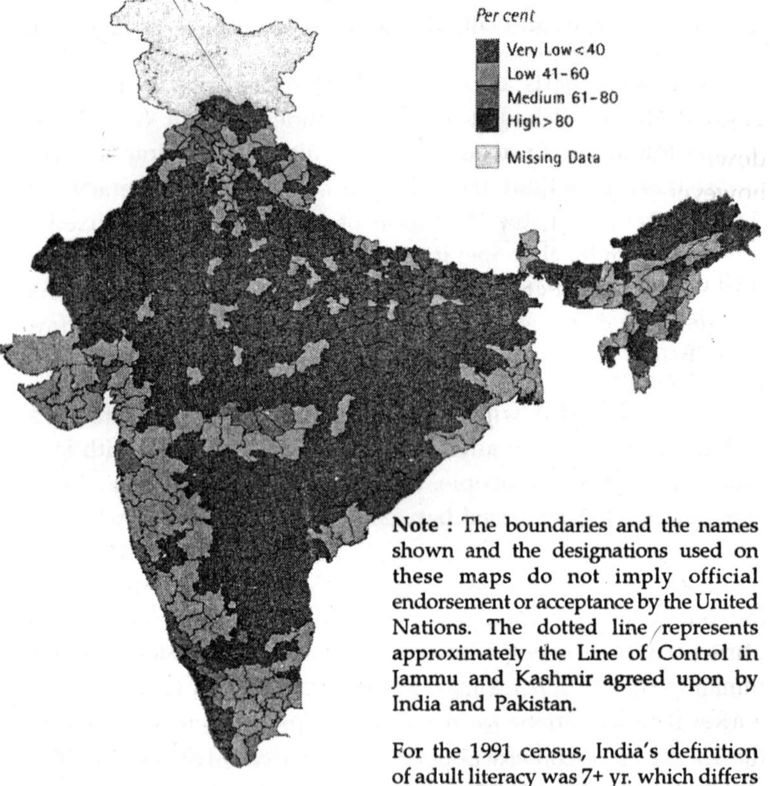

Note : The boundaries and the names shown and the designations used on these maps do not imply official endorsement or acceptance by the United Nations. The dotted line represents approximately the Line of Control in Jammu and Kashmir agreed upon by India and Pakistan.

For the 1991 census, India's definition of adult literacy was 7+ yr. which differs from the EFA data base of 15+ yr.

Source : Census 1991, Office of the Registrar General and Census Commissioner, Ministry of Home Affairs, India, 1991. Age Group: 7+ yr.

Severe problems of adult illiteracy cannot be solved through the formal structures that are being put in place for children. There are various responses: reliance on voluntary and non-government organisations in all regions; the district as a base and mobilisation of civic society in India; a concerted interdepartmental campaign in Indonesia which is reported to have brought levels of the illiterate population (15-24 years of age) down to under 2 per cent in 1998; and intensive drives, mobilising all available resources in China.

The E9 synthesis report draws attention to the striking success of the Chinese efforts to reduce adult illiteracy rates from a high of 80 per cent in 1949 to 22.3 per cent in 1990. A further reduction over the Jomtien decade brought the figure for 1997 down to 16.4 per cent of those over 15—still a large absolute figure, however, given the size of China' population.

Thus, often in the face of great difficulty, determined and well organised efforts have brought about significant reductions in illiteracy rates. Countries report many examples of successful literacy training programmes, both public and private, from which much is being learnt for future campaigns. Most important is the need for consistent effort with the full engagement of the community supported by strong, well-resourced policies.

Lessons from the literacy drives

The conclusions drawn in the EFA 2000 Assessments about the outstanding problems in adult illiteracy are familiar and unsurprising. As in other dimensions of education for all, illiteracy remains greatest in rural areas and marginal urban areas. Poverty is a key issue and must be addressed. Groups and communities with the lowest levels of literacy need to understand its wider benefits and to become directly involved in campaigns, not the subjects of strategies devised on high and in remote centres of power.

In many countries, literacy levels of adult women, particularly in rural areas, remain lower than those of men. As girls' participation in primary schooling increases and as they continue to outperform boys, this pattern can be expected to change in the decades ahead. Meanwhile the direct involvement of women at the local level is essential and many grass roots projects have demonstrated its value. Co-operation among the various players, public and private, local and donor is often weak; it can be greatly improved. Policy priorities and coordination of cross-sectoral effort by governments are often inadequate to the task. Bureaucratic structures and engrained habits need to be reviewed as part of national commitments to achieve results. To-down strategies that fail to engage communities at a very local level and build on their motivation and interests don't work.

For each of the negative lessons, there is a positive correlate and an implicit target for the future. Where weaknesses persist-in retention rates and successful performance by children in primary (and secondary) schools-improvements are required if adult illiteracy levels are to be further reduced. Conversely, the best predictor of the learning achievement of children is the literacy and education level of their parents.

This underlines the importance of reform strategies that are comprehensive and systemic. Adult literacy, like adult education generally, needs to be interrelated with basic education reform strategies whose focus is the formal school system. As in other target areas, there is need for systematic monitoring and evaluation of the effectiveness and impact of non-formal literacy programmes.

Universalisation of basic education, where it has been achieved, leaves a concentration of high rates of illiteracy among adults who have lacked basic education in the past or regressed in literacy skills. This circumstance provides an opportunity for highly focused policy initiatives. In Latin American countries where participation rates in basic schooling have risen, there is a progressively greater focus of attention in literacy campaigns on the post-school population. But attention must be given to what children actually attain by way of literacy standards in school. Results on tests are falling well below age norms in many countries, as reported in the MLA studies of African and Arab states. Universalisation in the sense of enrolment and participation rates is not enough. The persistence of illiteracy among children in primary school is itself an indicator of future adult illiteracy.

Despite the enormous difficulties arising from the inadequate empirical base, lack of clarity in definitions and the different interpretative standpoints, several messages emerge from the assessment of the adult literacy target.

IMPROVEMENT OF LEARNING ACHIEVEMENT

TARGET DIMENSION: Improvement of learning achievement such that an agreed percentage of an appropriate age cohort (for example 80 per cent of 14 year olds) attains or surpasses a defined level of necessary learning achievement.

Putting 'achievement' on the map

During the nineties, further steps have been taken in many countries and through international projects to define and assess learning achievement. Individual countries and states within them have their own criteria of learning achievement and have many different ways of assessing and reporting it. There is growing interest in clearer definitions of performance and achievement and in the construction of age-grade norms ad other system-wide performance measures (17). In some countries—the United Kingdom for example—these norms are being used for target setting and in judgements about the quality of performance of schools and teachers. France has in place a comprehensive national system for assessing, reporting on and evaluating students' learning achievements. The Goals 2000 Project in the USA involves leading national and state political figures in setting national goals for primary and secondary education; it has led to national standards in curriculum subjects for assessing student learning outcomes. Standards have also been set for teachers and there is growing interest in defining achievement both for students and teachers according to what they can do, as well as what they know.

Several of the countries reporting on this target have given details of major reforms designed to monitor and bring about improvements in student achievement. The joint UNESCO-UNICEF project, Monitoring Learning Achievement (MLA) which was established in 1992 to monitor learning achievement around the world at the grade 4 level, has stimulated activity in more than 50 countries, and led to specific studies of the quality of children's learning in Africa, the Arab States, Latin America and Kazakhstan (18).

When framework statements on the purposes of education and on curriculum goals in a cross-section of countries are scanned, it quickly becomes evident that quite complex issues for assessing performance, quality and progress arise. These purposes and goals commonly include—in addition to a broad range of subject matter knowledge—competencies, personal qualities, ethical values, social skills, civic responsibility, physical development and health.

'Learning achievement' is not reducible to scores on cognitive tests. Over-reliance on examinations as a measure of student learning is heavily criticised in some country reports, but is very difficult to change. Long established and widely used assessment measures—sessional examinations of subject content mastery for screening purposes, teacher assessments of pupil performance and progress in specific curriculum topics and learning skills, and standardised pencil and paper tests-usually have a strong cognitive bias. This does not suit some students and of itself is insufficient as a measure of learning achievement for any student. In addition to the growing interest in defining minimum standards of cognitive attainment levels by age and grade, countries are also setting goals in terms of competencies and aptitudes which are believed to have a high labour market value and broader sets of life skills including learning readiness and capability. There is often an unresolved tension between these and formal examination and testing requirements.

Cognitive-oriented tests still tend to dominate school assessment, often reflecting heavy emphasis on a narrow range of skills in the practice of teaching. Several countries, China and Japan, for example, have expressed great concern over the grip that tests and examinations have on teachers, students and families. The measured levels of achievement are often very high but thought to be too narrow and to depend unduly on rote learning and memorisation. The national report from China makes the point quite starkly: 'how to cope with examinations obsesses the minds of students, teachers and school leadership'. The goals of basic education are thereby 'seriously distorted.' However to change this situation it is not enough just to reform examinations. New curricula, teaching materials, pedagogical practices and assessment procedures, are required, together with the reform of teacher education. As the author of the national report on China says, 'arduous tasks indeed'. But unless reforms of this nature are undertaken, not only in the examination-dominated countries, the sought-for improvement in the nature and quality of learning will not occur.

Various proxy measures are used in assessing learning achievement—levels of investment in education, survival and completion rates, gross enrolment ratios, student-teacher ratios, levels of teacher education, and the supply and quality of text books and other materials. On these indicators, there are big problems in many countries. In South Asia and Sub-Saharan Africa, less than three out of four enrolees reach grade 5. In the least developed countries taken together, only half reach this level and many drop out after the first or second grade. Student-staff ratios and levels of teacher education are poor in many countries (19). Results reported in many of the MLA Study reports raise serious questions about students' learning. While proxy measures and test scores tell only part of the story, together with concerns widely expressed in the reports, they indicate that most countries are still far from achieving what they themselves define as satisfactory learning outcomes.

The adoption, at Jomtien, of a target to improve learning achievement is of itself an important contribution to the international movement to focus on learning outcomes and on the quality of learning and teaching processes. As stated in the E9 report, 'At the end, what matters is whether students are learning what they need and should. To focus on learning, it is necessary to go beyond the formalities of school enrolment and rates of... [attendance], and to ascertain whether the students are acquiring knowledge that is useful for a productive and meaningful life.' (20)

How far, then, have countries been able to demonstrate in the EFA 2000 Assessment what students are learning, the value of that learning, and the progress that has been made in stengthening and improving learning in the decade since Jomtien? The tantalising answer is 'a little and yet a lot'. The reports give a variety of answers to these questions, mainly, however, they are fragmentary and in the form of directions that are being set and illustrative material on assessment policies and practices. Except for the Monitoring Learning Achievement project—which however is concentrated on only one grade level (4th grade primary)—relatively few data have emerged from the EFA 2000 Assessment, either on what students are learning or on learning outcomes. Nor is there much discourse on the personal and social value of what is being taught and learnt. On the other hand, there is a significant public interest, nationally and internationally, in the processes and results of assessment of student learning.

National policy statements for improving educational outcomes are commonplace. National assessment systems are becoming more common especially in economically advanced countries. New curriculum frameworks setting out broad sets of common learnings in Australia, Norway, Sweden, Japan, the Netherlands, the United Kingdom and Canadian provinces among many others have been constructed during the 90s. Many other countries either have in place or are strengthening their national and regional systems to assess what students are learning in school as indicated by the following examples: the National Elementary Achievement Test (NEAT) in the Philippines and the National Primary School Achievement Test (PSAT) in Malaysia; the national assessment of basic education in Brazil (SAEB) (mathematics, language and the main determinants of school achievement and failure); moves towards national standards and state level testing in India; new and additional mechanisms to measure prescribed student learning outcomes at the primary level and minimum competency testing in part of the Caribbean; measurements of children's learning achievements through the Southern African Consortium for the Measurement of the Quality of Education (SACMEQ); and the assessment of basic learning achievements at the grade 4 level in Africa, the Arab States, and Kazakhstan through participation in the UNESCO/UNICEF MLA project.

Building on the International Educational Achievement (IEA) studies over several decades, is a large scale and very influential study of student achievement in mathematics and science (TIMMS: the Third International Mathematics and Science Study). Further work of this nature, ultimately extending into other curriculum areas, has recently been launched by the OECD-PISA (Program for International Science Assessment) which is expected to involve many countries in addition to OECD members.

A general conclusion to be drawn from the results of these and other assessment programmes is that there are very large within-country differences, often greater than the between-country differences which are the ones that attract most media interest. This is to underline a recurring theme of this Report: gross inequality of learning opportunities and unevenness of outcomes within single jurisdictions, which nevertheless often have the capacity to redress imbalances.

In addition to the findings on student learning outcomes, the national and international assessment programmes have become a vehicle for training personnel. As a result of the massive publicity they attract through the 'league tables' favoured by journalists and editors, there is also a greatly increased public awareness of the work of educational institutions and teachers.

These and other procedures—recently introduced, well-established or still in the planning stage—point to an intention to get a better grip on what students are learning and how well teachers and schools are performing. An issue that has come to the fore in the publicity given to the reports on student learning outcomes is the variability of conditions affecting learning. Initially, these conditions were widely ignored in crude comparisons and ranking. Attention drawn to the contrasts between poorer and richer regions and schools, teacher capabilities, resources for learning, family and community backgrounds and so forth has exploded the myths of 'equal opportunity' and 'a level playing field' without, as yet, subduing the impulse to make glib comparisons. Further analyses of student learning environments and conditions affecting learning is therefore required—and to some extent is being undertaken—to pinpoint and explain gross outcome differences. Although still in relatively early stages in most countries, this line of inquiry will facilitate policy refinement and the fine tuning of resource allocation and such remedial procedures as may be required.

It is clear that in the 90s there has been significant improvement in many countries in methods used to determine learning outcomes and the factors that help to explain differences. It is rather surprising, therefore, that so little data on learning outcomes has been provided in the reports. Proxy measures, which are only partly satisfactory, have had to be resorted to in order to gain some insights into learning achievement. Net enrolment rates, years of schooling, teacher-pupil ratios, levels of teachers' education and others are included in the **Statistical Document.** But what are students learning and how well are they performing?

So little of a systematic kind has been reported in the EFA 2000 Assessments on learning outcomes that achievement of this

Jomtien target remains largely unknown. Clearly this is unsatisfactory. For future work both the target itself and ways of ascertaining progress will need careful consideration. There must be a review of the data issue: what kinds of information exist and how might they best be assembled? What further steps are needed to get a grip on what students know and can do? What are the most successful ways of improving learning outcomes?

Individual countries often have records of trends in student performance including results in public examinations and test scores, and they might be pieced together to provide single country or within-country profiles. There is no immediate prospect of large scale international studies covering the whole range of student learning or even the full gamut of what are deemed to be core or essential learnings. But there is plenty of scope for countries to improve their own procedures for monitoring and assessing student learnings, for sample and case studies to pinpoint specific issues like urban-rural differences, and for an improved international exchange of experiences. For example, further progress can be made in harmonising the relationship between enrolment and quality of learning and teaching through the national and international efforts of the Latin American Educational Quality Assessment Laboratory (Laboratorio) and the Southern African Consortium for Measuring Educational Quality (SACMEQ).

Several reports do provide brief and indirect assessments of learning outcomes, but there is little encouragement to be drawn from them. The cautious conclusions drawn in the synthesis report of the Asia-Pacific region perhaps best typify the overall situation wherever participation and external conditions are unfavourable: 'Pupil teacher ratios and survival rates are sometimes used as proxies for learning quality. In the present case there is almost no reliable trend data concerning learning achievement that are based on measurement using comparable instruments and procedures. To that extent it may be said that the burden of the evidence suggests that there are, in many countries, problems of quality in the primary cycle'. (21).

Many countries note weaknesses in the academic and professional expertise of teachers and the conditions under which they work. Projects in Malawi, Sudan and the Syrian Republic focus on improving the quality of teaching in rural areas; skilled teachers are being redeployed form urban to rural areas in Guinea, higher entry requirements are being set in Egypt and the Libyan Arab Jamarihiya; most countries in Latin America and the Caribbean are moving towards incentives to attract and retain teachers; in Pakistan the Northern Areas Education Project is bringing in additional teachers to meet needs in deprived areas. Improvements in teacher education are seen as essential for speeding up the pace of reform in China's 1999 'Action Scheme for Invigorating Education Towards the 21st Century'. These are among many initiatives being taken to improve the quality and supply of teachers.

Inferences and conclusions about learning outcomes

It seems clear that very few countries have in practice set themselves the Jomtien learning target, let alone recorded measurable gains against it. For many countries, the conclusion is inescapable; in the words of the Arab Framework for Action: 'Quality education is still a privilege for a few' (22). From a global perspective, this means, first, too few countries and, second, that within all countries there are differences, often very big ones, between an education of good quality enjoyed by the minority and a considerably lower and more variable quality of educational experience for the majority. So long as serious inadequacies and inequalities in provision, access and learning opportunities remain, for reasons of both socio-economic efficiency and equity there should be renewed efforts to establish clear, realistic and relevant targets. Equally, programmes are needed to focus on specified difficulties. Transparent reporting mechanisms should be put in place.

Those countries that are setting age/grade based standards of learning achievement have at least established frameworks for such assessments. When there is universal participation in schooling of medium to long duration and systems of monitoring over time are in place, it will be possible in the next stage of EFA to produce and use internationally comparable data of much greater descriptive and analytic value than exist now. Many countries are not in a position now to produce such data. For them a more immediate task is to define realisable quality targets and ways of achieving them.

EXPANSION OF PROVISION OF BASIC EDUCATION AND TRAINING IN OTHER ESSENTIAL SKILLS REQUIRED BY YOUTH AND ADULTS

TARGET DIMENSION: Expansion of provision of basic education and training in other essential skills required by youth and adults, with programme effectiveness assessed to terms of behavioural change and impact on health, employment and productivity.

A widening agenda

The movement to orient both formal and informal education of youth and adults more towards generic learning, broadly defined competencies and 'life skills' has gained in momentum since the 80s. Strongly driven by a mixture of labour market changes and concern over social cohesion, this movement has brought in its train a large number of projects to improve skills and raise motivation. It has influenced national education goals statements, resulting in government-funded programmes, and is prominent in statements and recommendations from business round tables, representatives of industry, trade unions and other NGOs. Likewise, it has featured throughout the 90s in declarations and conferences organised by regional and global bodies.

New national qualifications frameworks have been established to: facilitate the recording and the analysis of skills and competencies; define appropriate learning experiences and setting; and regulate and interrelate qualifications that attest to competence. Although relatively little is known about the skill level of large segments of the population in many countries, this situation is changing, through surveys, funded research and the use of various proxy measures, including attendance and completion rates especially in vocationally-oriented programmes, and placement on the labour market. Changes, especially in secondary schools and vocational programmes, together with better health care and welfare services are contributing to improvements in human capital. But youth joblessness, the incidence of low-skilled jobs and mismatches between basic education and training and the labour market continue to cause concern. Major gaps and weaknesses are observable; they are particularly acute in Africa, large parts of Asia and Central and South America but are also apparent in Europe, North America and Australasia.

Several international organisations, notably the European Union, the OECD, the ILO, UNESCO, the World Bank and several national agencies have played leading roles in assisting efforts regionally and within countries to define competencies and skills, determine the learning experiences appropriate to them and establish, strengthen and analyse linkages between the labour market and education and training providers. Other international bodies have played similar roles in relation to health, welfare and other behavioural domains. Funded projects are common; but they fall far short of the need and have often proved to make only a moderate impact.

The range of variables in this target area is wide and there is a lack of data on behavioural change. Together with the diversity of agencies and organisations with a degree of responsibility or interest, these factors have meant that the authors of the EFA 2000 Assessment Country Reports found it exceedingly difficult to draw conclusions. The activities relevant to skills development, health, employment and productivity fall outside the scope of any one ministry and involve the non-government sector, communities and enterprises and the media. They are seldom systematically monitored. Too often they consist of a succession of short-term interventions which lack strategic significance. Public funding for out-of-school youth, where available on any scale, comes from a considerable diversity of sources. Governments often lack the incentive as well as the capacity to coordinate activities and produce cohesive policies and strategies. Skills development and behavioural change in youth are essential for sustainable development but there is a dearth of information on programmes that have been successful in these respects. A better integration of activities, it is often suggested, would bring results but the EFA 2000 Assessments provide scant evidence of changes in this regard.

The programme areas that are receiving greatest attention vary by country and regions. In Western Europe, and several other advanced economies, the decade of the 90s has been characterised by a continuing preoccupation with youth and adult unemployment. Numerous programmes have been introduced in schools and vocational training institutions to improve transition from education to working life. Innovative projects include those based in workplaces and run by private training companies. Guidance and services for labour market placement have been increased and improved. The major objective has been to better equip people for labour market participation. An underlying concern is that unless better results can be achieved, social cohesion is seriously threatened. Programmes, targeted mainly at early school leavers ad those whose school performance has been modest, are being extended through the orientation of school curricula to the world of work (23).

In African countries, formal vocational preparation is high on the policy agenda—but so also are reproductive health and family planning, the fight against AIDS, hygiene and health education and extending primary education, and literacy. Youth unemployment rates are often extremely high and with weak economies and no clear orientation for future labour market growth, programme effectiveness is often questionable.

In several South American countries—Bolivia, Colombia and Ecuador among them—curriculum development and assessment are being directed towards skills acquisition in line with international policy trends that favour less attention to the mastery of pre-specified content and greater emphasis on active learning, participatory methodologies and 'learning how to learn'.

Countries in the Asia-Pacific region report mass programmes which aim to improve the skill level of the workforce. Among them are: expanding the capacity of institutions and improving labour market skills in the Malaysian Sixth Plan; improved literacy rates and educational standards in Lao PDR; private and public programmes for Training in Essential Skills in Indonesia; vocational training for targeted groups including the disabled in Cambodia. In the reports of the Trans-Caucasus and Central Asian States and Mongolia, vocational schools and colleges, technical schools and tertiary institutions are seen as the principal vehicles for work-oriented skills training, but in several countries resource flows to education and training institutions have been seriously disrupted. In some countries, e.g. in Western Europe and Australasia, in addition to the preparatory phase, there is a marked emphasis on skills formation for young unemployed people and on the continuing upgrading and professional development of the workforce. (24)

It is most regrettable that, in the regional syntheses, so few data are presented on this important area. Many countries have either not contributed at all or have provided only very sketchy information. The argument that control of the HIV/AIDS pandemic, for example, depends on education is but one of many reasons for paying more attention to behavioural outcomes, difficult as they may be to measure or ascertain. The concept of a 'healthy lifestyle' is behavioural, as is civic responsibility and job capability. The challenge to identify 'behavioural change' is very demanding and indeed thus far seems to be unrealistic on any systematic basis. For both this target area and the one that follows, there is need for serious reflection and more creative thinking at Dakar. What are the best, practical indices of behavioural change and how can countries move forward in developing them and monitoring performance accordingly?

What does stand out in the reports in this target area is the growth of provision—both formal and non-formal, publicly and privately financed—for labour market preparation. There is a great variety of programmes but relatively little evaluation of their effect, e.g. behavioural changes and impact on health, employment and productivity. Research studies on particular groups and settings throw some light and there is a strong conviction internationally among policy analysts that, for example, productivity improvements are highly correlated with advanced levels of skills training, not only in the new technologies, but also with such attributes as team spirit and capabilities in problem solving.

The reports on this target provide insufficient data for conclusions about either positive gains or significant set-backs. The EFA 2000 Assessment was intended to be inter-ministerial but it seems that there has been very little input, in many countries from the relevant ministries other than education. For this as for several other target areas it will be essential in the next phase to again seek closer co-operation across ministries if cross-sectoral programmes are to emerge and data be produced on outcomes.

KNOWLEDGE, SKILLS AND VALUES REQUIRED FOR BETTER LIVING AND SOUND AND SUSTAINABLE DEVELOPMENT

TARGET: Increased acquisition by individuals and families of the knowledge, skills and values required for better living and sound and sustainable development, made available through all education channels including the mass media, other forms of modern and traditional communication, and social action, with effectiveness assessed in terms of behavioural change.

Quality of life

Many countries combined their returns on 'better living' with those on 'life skills'. Partly this is because data are extremely limited on both, but also because there is not a clear differentiation between the two target areas-unless life skills' were to be taken firmly in the direction of education and training for work, and 'better living' in the direction of overall quality of life and standard of living, health and well-being. 'Health', however, was allocated to target area 5 and the concept of behavioural change has relevance alike to the sixth and the fifth target areas.

For the purpose of this Report, the ideas of quality of life and well being will serve as the primary orientation for target area six. The summary of 'basic learning needs' required by human beings as set forth in the Jomtien Declaration, and reformulated in the Sub-Saharan Africa synthesis provides a concise starting point for considering 'better living' and 'sustainable development'.

Through the satisfaction of the basic learning needs defined at Jomtien and reformulated in the South and East African regional synthesis report, individuals would both be empowered and assume a responsibility.

- to respect and build upon their collective cultural, linguistic and spiritual heritage;
- to promote the education of others, to further the cause of social justice, to contribute to environmental protection;
- to be tolerant toward social, political and religious systems which differ from their own, ensuring that commonly accepted humanistic values and human rights are upheld;
- to work for international peace and solidarity in an interdependent world.

The foregoing sets of needs, qualities, attributes and responsibilities provide a general, highly optimistic backcloth to all six target areas. They also cover a large part of the territory occupied by national education goals statements in many parts of the world. But they have a specific reference to the 'better living' theme of the sixth target area.

As with the fifth target area it is not possible to produce a trend analysis of the Jomtien decade such that there can be clearcut conclusions about gains made, losses sustained and behavioural changes experienced. For one thing, although there may be widespread agreement on a list of behavioural correlates, their particular interpretation will vary according to cultural and personality differences and value preferences; for another 'better living' is an open ended concept and a creative process whereby individual and collective experience will constantly throw up new dimensions and possibilities. Then again, in recognition of these considerations, countries seemed to find great difficulty in reporting progress, as distinct from the difficulties and obstacles standing in the way of the whole EFA enterprise. Before coming to country statements, however, it is necessary to refer again to those environmental factors, underlying conditions and change forces which, in many parts of the world, bring into question the capacity to achieve or sustain 'better life'.

Some parts of the world and some sectors of the community have enjoyed substantial gains in living standards in the nineties. But for others, conditions are no better, indeed they often are worse, Community-and life-destroying natural disasters, acute civil disorder, economic mismanagement and corruption, rampant disease, substance abuse, malnutrition and hunger, poverty, injustice and inequities are conditions for 'worse living' for large numbers of people. Discriminatory access to education and training, ineffectual literacy programmes, outmoded curricula and assessment practices, chronic underfunding, shortage of equipment and materials, poor teaching and lack of family and community support are not factors that lay the foundation in people's lives for better living or the sustainable development of communities. The increasing gaps between better off and worse off countries and groups and individuals within countries are an additional force undermining the universalistic principles of distributive justice and ethical relations among people and nations adopted at Jomtien. Unfortunately whole countries and regions have been afflicted in these ways during the 90s.

The five Jomtien targets that precede the sixth and the strategies considered appropriate to them, together with the positive action taken during the Jomtien decade, constitute a world-wide programme designed to achieve a better living for hundreds of millions if not billons of people. It scarcely needs arguing that several years of primary schooling of good quality instead of economically forced child labour and premature motherhood is 'better living'. It is, thus, properly the appraisal of the Jomtien movement as a whole and its role in the promotion of education for all and not of the sixth target area in isolation that is required in drawing conclusions about the achievement of 'better life' for all.

Perhaps it was this realisation that led so few countries to comment separately and concretely on the sixth target area. Many of them, in drawing lessons from the decade and in formulating ideas for the future, implicitly if not explicitly offered their commentaries on whether or not gains have been made in 'better living'.

'Better living' has connotations of virtue and moral worth, of taking pleasure in and gaining happiness from doing the 'right' things—hence a moral component. For educators and all those concerned with sustainable development there appear to be several inbuilt criteria. These include, for example, efforts in Indonesia, Malaysia and the Philippines to sustain rich cultural heritages, teaching in indigenous languages, using local resources and materials, ensuring that local and diverse communities have an impact on what is taught, and incorporating natural history and culture in the curriculum.

In the Latin-American sub regional report, a set of 'better living' themes are listed:

- respect for the dignity of human life, constructing a culture of peace;
- strengthening of democracy and respect for human rights;

- development of a full, affective family and sexual life;
- adoption of healthy lifestyles;
- affirmation of equal rights and respect for ethnic and cultural diversity;
- respect and care for the environment;
- respect for one's own and other's cultural inheritance.

These themes, given different weight in different countries are pursued through a wide range of educational activities and organisations, both formal and non-formal.

Considering links between schooling and worthwhile pursuits, the authors of the Caribbean synthesis state that children should develop not just competence in but 'a love for reading', and a readiness to see in reading a 'recreational activity' and television as a 'medium for pertinent, focused curriculum information through the ever popular school quiz'. But reading materials and the mass media often have no educative purpose whatsoever. Their uptake and impact for example on levels of violence and anti-social behaviour, raise value questions which few countries or organisations seemed prepared to take up reporting for the EFA 2000 Assessment.

'Sustainable development', as the report on Sub-Saharan Africa points out, must start with acknowledgement of the immense diversity of life styles reflecting factors of land form, ecology, settlement patterns, agriculture, extractive and manufacturing industry, trade and transportation and others. 'Sustainable' does not evoke a uniform response or provision: what is a 'better life' for a mountain mining community is not in all respects the same as for city dwellers, desert nomads or intensively cultivated plantation regions, although basic needs and rights may be identical. This suggests a need for considerable flexibility not so say creativity in translating broadly defined education and development targets into relevant, successful action programmes on the ground.

The sixth Jomtien target refers to the mass media and other forms of modern and traditional communication, and social action. Various uses of media in education are referred to in many country reports, for example, distance education in island communities (Tuvalu, Cook Islands, Nauru, Tonga) and in the Latin American sub-regional report. Radio is widely used, and commended as a cost effective medium by the authors of the special study on New Technologies and Cost-Effective Delivery System. Very large scale distance education operations have become widespread in parts of Asia, North America and Australia, mainly for adults. A wider consideration is that use of media for non-formal and informal education opens up a vast territory – not only mass media but also the arts, religion, recreation and sporting, activities and community groups. The Fijian report, for example, refers to a campaign by the Ministry of Youth for changing attitudes and motivation, through sports and music programmes for unemployed, rural youth. But the scope and scale of reporting on these and other forms of communication and social action has proved far too great for most countries to be incorporated into the EFA 2000 Assessments. It is not surprising that there are so few references to these domains, although some countries emphasise the promotion of local and traditional culture through song, dance festivals (Belize), the church (Tonga) and collections of oral literature (Eritrea).

The uses of electronic and print media in the formation and education for youth and adults and in improving the quality of life has scarcely featured in the reports. The target as at present worded is too all encompassing. The conclusion in inescapable: if this target direction were to be retained, it should be reformulated to achieve a better focus and enable manageable procedures for monitoring and appraisal. Value issues arising from use of the term 'better living' inevitably arise once the stage of bare subsistence is passed. These will not be easy to accommodate and will require an extensive cross-cultural dialogue.

In the regional report on the countries of Western Europe and North America, 'better living' is captured in the term 'prosperity'. This does not mean just material prosperity – although economic growth is a byword in the policies of these countries – it refers equally to the uses to which economic growth is put and the criteria for distributing and sharing the benefits of economic growth. In this regard, and beginning in the late 90s an increase in aid to poorer countries or at least a restoration of the earlier cuts, and debt relief programmes signal renewed attentiveness to the 'better living' needs of large parts of the world. Current 'Jubilee 2000' proposals for debt cancellation and for a focus on social sector expenditures including health and education are most welcome. The thematic study on the work of Donor Agencies underlines the scale of the task to provide conditions for 'better living' for hundreds of millions of people.

Efforts to reduce or control the large scale environmental degradation that have ensued from industrialisation, urbanisation and short sighted agricultural practices and deforestation, are examples of moves to take 'sustainable development' seriously. These and other topics relevant to better life have been the subject of the sequence of world conferences in the 90s listed in the Appendix. But that does into mean an end to environmental degradation. Education and health programmes of the right kind have an important role to play in shifting attitudes and improving knowledge and capability.

The adverse effects on smaller and poorer countries of globalisation and the lack of balance between multilateral corporation and weak or small national economies means that 'better living' for some countries and groups is being achieved at the expense of others. These forces are not beyond human control and social action. Mounting worldwide concern is having some impact, through political action and international processes.

Several change forces in the wider environment can have positive implications for achieving the EFA targets. Yet few of the reports make any attempt in comments on the sixth Jomtien target to interrelate these wider contextual environmental considerations and educational policy and practice.

In education, on a wide front there have to be both targeting and movements. There must be constant referral to the relationships among educational and other policies, practice on the ground and the changing environmental forces. These relationships are receiving a lot of attention in some fora. In discussion about any possible further development of this sixth target dimension in the next phase of EFA work, these relationships would have to be more adequately explored than they have been to date.

It is unsatisfactory that a target dimension should be specified but in such a way that countries were either unable or unwilling to provide responses of any substance. The combination of the amorphous concept of 'better living', the mass media and behavioural changes in one target dimension is implausible. Yet the attempt to marry educational process and outcomes to quality of life and to assess the value of mass media as instruments of education is inescapable in any broader consideration of what education is for and the many ways in which it can be provided. One difficulty arises from a failure to draw upon such international procedures as exist for operationalising 'better life'. Such procedures do exist, even if surrounded by controversy, for example, in the UNDP quality of life indicators. From an economic perspective there is also the whole system of national accounts and the indicators of economic performance prepared, negotiated and used by several international organisations (IMF, World Bank, OECD, etc).

While it may prove difficult to draw from these diverse sources some commonly agreed measures of 'better life' or 'prosperity', continued reference to the concepts in this target dimension will require a much more searching analysis of just how it is to be defined, implemented, monitored and assessed.

The mass media and other forms of communication as instruments of education probably required separate treatment, drawing on the expertise available in a range of culturally focused disciplines, cross-disciplinary media studies, ethnography, communications science, psychology, education and others.

Without a well coordinated intellectual effort, drawing these and other disciplines together, it is difficult to see how there can be progress on either implementing this element of the sixth target dimension or reporting progress on what is being achieved.

Strategic Plans and Legal Measures

In **Mexico,** a National Agreement for the Modernization of Basic Education, in 1992, constitutional reforms and a new education law, in 1993, set the framework. The most important reform was the decentralization of basic education and teacher education. The broad goals, definition of contents evaluation and compensatory policies were retained by central government, while administration of the operation of education institutions was for the states. Social mobilization occurred through participatory councils. Compensatory policies for poorer communities were introduced and special attention given to bi-lingual education.

In **Brazil,** a ten year Education for All plan was established for the period 1993-2003. It was strengthened by: a constitutional amendment which reorganised basic education funding to improve equity and earmarked more resources for education; a new National Education Law including new evaluative procedures; a new National Plan referred to the Congress for approval in 1998.

In **China** a new Five-year Plan for Educational Development and Long Rang Development Towards the year 2000 was established, shifting the focus from universal primary education to universal 9 year compulsory schooling. This was supported by central regulations and guidelines. Numerous measures were introduced to speed up universal primary schooling either in full or 3-4 year programmes in remote areas and to improve provision for girls, the disabled and the children of migrants.

Contd...

In Pakistan, targets were set in National Education Policy 1998-2010 for universal enrolment and compulsory attendance and a completion rate in primary schools of 80 per cent, public-private partnership, decentralised management, assessment of basic competencies and increased levels of investment.

(Source : S. Schwartzman: **Education for All: the Nine Largest Countries.** March 2000).

In Papua New Guinea a National Plan was adopted in 1995 following legislative changes. It is progressively displacing older, much criticised piecemeal educational arrangements with a new, integrated 12 year national system together with upper secondary vocational, tertiary and adult education. The objectives include higher participation, survival and transition rates, more relevant curricula, a better gender balance, lower unit costs and improved management and administration.

(Source : EFA Assessment: **Papua New Guinea)**

Early Childhood Care and Education Comes into Focus

Recognition of the importance of improvements in early childhood care and education has grown in the 90s:

- Environmental changes, some quite disastrous, like civil war and HIV/AIDS, have increased awareness of the needs of infants and young children and threats to their well being;
- Major advances have been made in reducing infant and child mortality;
- Gains have occurred in knowledge and understanding of development in early childhood including learning capabilities and needs;

Contd...

- Political and community leaders, funding bodies, planners and the public at large have become more conscious of the benefits of early support and intervention to facilitate learning;
- The have been major educational reforms, laws and regulations relating to early childhood care and education; the overall level of international financing available for early childhood care and education has increased;
- Better coordination of policies and the exercise of responsibility has occurred in some countries.

But lack of financial and human resources, weak organisational capacity, other priorities believed to be more urgent, and community attitudes help to explain little or no progress in many countries or regions.

(Source : R. G. Myers: **Early Childhood Care and Development. A Global Review, February, 2000.**)

Changing Patterns of Early Childhood Care and Education

For early childhood care and education, in all societies there is a timeless tradition of mother and family care, still seen by large numbers of people as preferable to away from home care and formal education. Increasingly, as other considerations impinge—decline of the extended family, family mobility and break-up, working mothers, advances in medical and social knowledge and urbanisation among them—what may still be regarded as preferable ceases to be a realistic option. Organised provision then must be made, not only for purposes of disease control, nutrition and psycho-social well being, but for structured learning as well. The latter is now being strongly reinforced (if still controversially) by research findings and conclusions drawn from neuroscience and cognitive psychology and applied to learning processes in early childhood.

Key Outcomes:

- Early childhood care and education has now been placed quite firmly on the global agenda;
- There is a growing acceptance of the value of ECCE and the need for better provision and qualitative improvements;
- Widespread acceptance of the value of maternal care, health and nutritional services is not matched in many countries by an adequate supply;
- Provision in early years education across and within countries is extremely diverse in respect of purposes and objectives, structures, organisation, starting age and length of programmes, facilities and personnel;
- Legislation and regulatory frameworks have been put in place and are an important stimulus to action;
- While there are very significant, rapid increases in enrolments in education facilities in several countries and steady growth in others, in poorer countries and regions there is generally very limited provision;
- Inequality of access and opportunity continue to favour families and children in urban centres;
- Increasing demand is being met through a mixture of public and private sources of support, control and management; NGOs and community groups play crucial roles;
- In only a few countries is there satisfaction with the quality of curricula, learning resources, teacher preparation and qualification;
- There have been—and are projected—big increases in international financing of ECCE;

Contd...

- Developments over the decade in monitoring, evaluation, and research are providing much improved data for policy making;
- Recognition is growing of the need for policy coherence and better co-operation across sectors.

Non-completion and Dropout of School

- Enrolment figures in primary schooling countries need to be read in conjunction with those on length of schooling and completion rates. In India and notwithstanding big improvements over the decade, lack of capacity by schools to retain children has been a serious problem, especially in the upper primary years and for girls (EFA 2000 Assessment Report, India)
- Although in the USA enrolment and school completion rates compare favourably with those in other industrial countries, a substantial minority of students—about one in 20—dropout of school at the middle and high school levels. 'The figures are a matter of concern because high school dropouts have lower earnings, experience more unemployment, and are more likely to end up needing public support, going to prison, and becoming pregnant than their peers who have a diploma' (Fiske and O'Grady, p. 18).

Poverty is Not the Only Issue

Generally, and across all of the regions, wherever enrolment and participation levels remain low, the major but not the only factor referred to in explaining failure or inability to meet target enrolment goals set by the governments themselves is the generic concept of poverty. The weakness of national economies—including inflationary pressures, the increased demands resulting from population growth and the poverty of a large proportion

Contd...

of the population, and accumulated national debt—are major impediments. Unless they are addressed there can be little hope of significant improvements in education. Domestic poverty or hardship, for example, in many countries stand in the way of the increases now sought for in family contributions to schooling. The opportunity coast of child labour is a major factor with poor families.

But questions must be asked as to whether governments have devoted a sufficient/rising proportion of their funds to meet the commitments entered into at Jomtien. Some have; others have not. To this issue must be added management of education budgets, including the ways in which national and regional budgets are apportioned to different sectors and the efficient use of resources. Big improvements in macro and micro policies in a number of countries are required if there is to be an adequate flow of funds to support universal primary education and effective utilisation of resources. Universal provision and access is within the capacity of all countries to deliver. A mix of economic and education reforms, implemented with great determination, can achieve this.

Interactions between Education and Population Trends

Educated women tend to have fewer children; when fertility rates decline and conditions are relatively stable, there are better opportunities to provide facilities for child upbringing care and early education and mothers' education. Educated parents also tend to make better use of health care facilities. In general, population decreases favour improved education, health and care of children. But this is not always the case. The impact of crises such as HIV/AIDS can be completely distorting—of demographic trends and policies for health improvement and education—with serious cost implications, for example for the medical care of teachers and their replacement.

(Source : R. G. Myers **Early Childhood Care and Development. A Global Review 1990-1999**; M. T. Siniscalco, **Achieving Education for All: Demographic Challenges**)

Non-formal Education to Meet the Needs of Out-of-School Children

Recognising the need to provide new ways of reaching marginalised groups, non-formal programmes have been launched by governments, local communities and NGOs in India. The programmes are condensed, use curricula and materials similar to those in the formal system, are delivered through part-time teaching including volunteers, at a time and place convenient to learners, and use village and local community facilities. The increased participation of voluntary agencies including NGOs in the 90s is described as 'phenomenal': and there have been big increases in the number of centres, enrolments and investment of financial and human resources. Flexibility and variety in the design and delivery of education are features which, together with qualitative improvement, will continue to be sought. This scheme is not a low cost alternative to primary schools, but a complementary approach to meet special needs.

Has the target been achieved?

- There have been spectacular improvements in access and participation rates in some countries in the Asia- Pacific region, good improvement in others and little if any change, or even regression in some; universal participation still remains a distant goal in many countries;
- Major inequities continue: urban/rural; gender; socio-economic; people with disabilities; working children; ethnic groups;
- There is need for more creative and innovative ways of providing opportunity for those who are excluded. The major issues included: commitment and strong policy leadership; base funding; the supply of trained teachers and teaching-learning materials; population increases and movement of people; warfare and civil disturbance;

Contd...

- Attrition is of growing concern including dropout, non completion and failure rates which remain high to very high in many systems of primary and secondary education;
- Completion of primary education is no longer regarded as a sufficient criterion for basic education in many countries which are treating a full secondary education and even some form of post-secondary or tertiary education as the essential basis for action, social and economic life and continuing learning.

Literacy Goals

To reduce and ultimately eliminate illiteracy, programmes aim to:

- reduce the total number of illiterate people as populations continue to expand;
- improve literacy rates for specific age bands and groups in society;
- ensure that literacy achieved in the school years is not lost;
- use literacy as a lever for social, cultural and economic advancement
- at the same time set higher standards of performance as broader concepts of literacy and literate cultures emerge.

The Focus on Adult Literacy Must Also Involve Children and their Schooling

Universal access to basic schooling and literacy training for children cannot be overlooked when reviewing adult literacy rates. Looking to the future, it is extremely important to bring

Contd...

children's literacy into the equation. Problems of large and varied geographical regions and diverse cultural expectations, inadequate schooling in poor and remote areas and lack of suitable programmes and facilities for linguistic and cultural minorities are among the existing factors, which are storing trouble for the future. The pool of adult illiteracy should not be enlarged by inflows of illiterate children who have either not attended school at all or have had only minimal and inadequate schooling.

A Sample of Latin American Literacy Initiatives

- In **Brazil,** the Solidarity Action Literacy Training Programme for young people and adult is sponsored by state and municipal governments, the private sector and NGOs.
- In **Ecuador,** the 'Monseñor Leonides Proano' National Literacy Campaign mobilises support from universities, the judiciary, churches, the armed forces, secondary schools, community organisations and volunteers.
- In **EL Salvador,** literacy training programmes or projects have been targeted on women, people in prison and displaced civil war refugees; they have been supported by UNESCO, UNDP, Cooperaión Española, and the European Community.
- In **Guatemala,** programmes have been delivered through a network of governmental and non-governmental agencies.
- In **Paraguay,** the Ministries of Education and Culture, Agriculture and Livestock, Justice, and Labor, Public Health and Social Welfare, and Defence offer literacy courses as do NGOs.

Source : Latin America Sub-regional Report. pp.39-40

Literacy Messages

- The data bases are so inadequate as to require a much greater effort at systematisation if firm conclusions and reliable inferences are to be drawn and if coherent policies are to be developed and implemented; audits are need to ensure open and honest reporting;
- There is a general consensus that in many countries there is slow and steady, sometimes spectacular improvement in reported literacy rates; better data would enable more reliable conclusions to be drawn about trends;
- Long standing disparities and inequities remain within countries; there is need for better focused equity target; the poorest countries, the poorest regions and the poorest groups are not receiving adequate support, although the are targets of several donors and aid agencies; in the least developed countries 1:2 adults are still illiterate.
- Adult literacy and non-formal education more generally are in many countries accorded insufficient priority and are at the margins of reform efforts;
- Successful programmes depend upon a variety of conditions: mobilising many and varied resources, local, national and intranational; sound organisation and persistence of activity often over long periods; community involvement and leadership; and attention to the life conditions of illiterate people and to their motivation and incentives to become fully literate;
- Policies for adult literacy need to take account of problems being experienced by school age children and the literacy standards they attain;
- Literacy of the most rudimentary kind is a useful intermediate target, as a step towards a broadly defined culture of literacy;
- Regular, reliable reporting of performance on agreed targets of basic literacy enable concentration on the most difficult problems and areas of greatest need.

Messages on Learning Achievement

- There are, at present, no internationally agreed indicators of learning achievement across the curriculum; such measures as do exist are mainly of a small number of school subjects and only a minority of countries participate in these studies;
- The data on learning outcomes prepared for the EFA 2000 Assessment are extremely limited, even nebulous. Inferences need to be drawn from diverse sources and can only be of a very general nature. Future work need to be much more systematic in defining relevant data sources and drawing them together. This might include analysis of the results of national and international studies of learning achievements; sample studies and case studies of specific topics including assessment methods used in schools and pedagogical practice;
- In countries where school enrolments fall well short of 100 per cent of the age group, learning achievements for the cohort as a whole are modest although they can be very high for selected groups;
- Significant inequalities of access and provision-for girls, disadvantaged groups, ethnic minorities, children in rural and remote locations and so on, result in very wide within-country disparities in learning outcomes for children of school age;
- Low rates of retention and survival in school and high rates of grade repeating especially in combination with low participation rates, and large numbers of untrained or semi-trained personnel, result in a low average standard of learning;
- Very high student-staff ratios in combination with inadequate school buildings and teaching/learning resources are generally (but not inevitably) associated with poor learning outcomes for large numbers of children;

Contd...

- Very high repetition rates are an indication not of high standards, but of a low quality of teaching and learning;
- Very low levels of public expenditure on schooling, irregularities in payments and other inefficiencies are associated with mediocre to weak student performance and low levels of learning outcomes;
- There are too few improvements worldwide in the supply of well trained teachers and their further professional development, and in their conditions of service and salaries;
- There is an urgent need to set clear, realistic and attainable targets for the standards of student learning in all countries, to carry out regular monitoring, and to deploy well targeted strategies for improvement.

Skills and other behavioural outcomes

- Very little is known from the EFA 2000 Assessment about the relation between skills development, desirable behavioural change and specific education and training programmes;
- Provision for the education and training of youth and adults in skills formation is increasing in scale, with growing emphasis on education in broadly defined competencies and 'life skills';
- The synergy among adult literacy, life skills and labour market capability is recognised in literacy projects in a number of countries;
- New partnerships have emerged between education providers, industry and community bodies;

Contd...

- New qualifications frameworks for recognition of a wide variety of learning and the award of qualifications are being established;
- Problems of youth unemployment and low levels of literacy and other skills are partly a consequence of inadequate education and training; increasingly they are seen as an economic hazard and a potential threat to social cohesion;
- Skills formation in youth and adults starting at school is widely recognised as a key to labour market reform and economic growth, but is still receiving little attention in many countries;
- The education and training needs of youth include health, hygiene, family planning, social and civic skills and continuing general education; narrow training is, however, still prevalent and is insufficient;
- There is often weak collaboration among ministries and insufficient co-ordination of diverse programmes.

Basic Learning Needs

Basic learning needs were defined at Jomtien and reformulated in the South and East African regional synthesis report prepared for the EFA 2000 Assessment:

- to be able to survive;
- to develop their full capacities to live and work in dignity;
- to participate fully in development;
- to improve the quality of their lives;
- to make informed decisions, and to continue learning.

What Have Been the Gains in 'Better Living'?

The overall Jomtien decade gains across all six target dimensions are gains in better living. Improved provision of early childhood education and care is a platform for lifelong learning and personal fulfilment; curricula, learning resources and teaching that are culturally sensitive build on and help sustain cultural heritage and facilitate personal growth; 'survival' and the quality of life are enhanced by improved health education, literacy and sound general and vocational preparation; increased opportunities for more education of good quality help lay the foundations of a better life, and so on. The gains in access and provision that have been recorded in statistics and discursive reports are gains in better living; the improvements recorded in retention rates, teacher education and training and so forth are gains in sustainable development. Where these gains are not made, 'living' may be no better and is often worse for large numbers of people. 'Better living' cultural and social themes feature in educational goals statements, curriculum designs and non-formal education programmes.

5

Outstanding Issues

The goals and targets set at Jomtien are broad and comprehensive. So much is expected and needed. Where to start, or where to focus when there is so much to be done? Among the topics of continuing debate internationally, as well as within countries, is the policy and financial priority to be afforded to different levels and stages of education. Another issue is the balance between public and private sources of support. Who should—or can—pay? Should investment be directed more towards formal pre-school education, primary schooling, adult literacy—or higher education and research? Are governments justified in seeking to shift the funding balance more towards local communities and families? Since rate of return analyses are frequently of a very general nature, or inconclusive, or impossible to conduct due to lack of data, the debate shifts to a complex set of social, political and educational issues.

Action on the ground is inevitably influenced by existing structures and provision and the difficulty of bringing about major shifts, for example in public budgets even when the will is strong. Educational change on any scale is almost always a slow and complex process requiring continuity of policy. The vital thing is to keep moving in a steady, purposive way, building on what has already been achieved.

Sometimes terminology has proved to be elusive or ambiguous, resulting in uneven reporting by countries on educational directions they are pursuing. The most striking example is the term 'basic education', which has a variety of references ranging from a specified number of years of primary schooling to lifelong learning, and from formal structures like classrooms and defined performance standards to informal, experiential learning. As societies become more complex, and technically advanced, as educational systems become more developed and inclusive, much more comes to be expected of 'basic' than a few years of compulsory schooling.

While there remain different interpretations of 'basic education' and 'education for all', and substantial variability in sources of information about what has been achieved, there is a general consensus about several major gains made in the course of the Jomtien decade. These have been discussed in previous chapters. At the same time, there is broad agreement on major outstanding issues which call for further attention. Some that have been identified in country and regional reports are best treated as specific to individual countries or regions. Others, however, reflect situations and requirements across a very large number of countries. There are five which stand out and call for further action by the international community:

- access and equity;
- quality, relevance and effectiveness;
- sharing responsibility;
- mobilizing resources;
- towards a new knowledge base.

ACCESS AND EQUITY

The **Convention on the Rights of the Child** gives added weight to the Universal Declaration of Human Rights and to the

EFA imperative that all children (people) have the right to learn at all stages of their development. The UNESCO **World Education Report 2000** has as its theme Education and Human Rights. The continuing need for declarations and reports on action—or inaction-is underlined by factors in the environment that abridge basic rights or undermine their achievement. Educators, and others directly responsible for child care and development have often felt powerless—but not completely—in the face of these forces. It is a great tribute to their humanity and professionalism that they continue regardless and that they have shown ways to make progress, at times against great odds.

Although ethically decisive in the modern world, the rights argument is not the only consideration weighing on countries. Arguments deriving from theories of human and social capital formation, the new growth theories in economics, and cost benefit analyses have been effective in demonstrating the very high economic and social costs to countries and regions within them of large numbers of uneducated, unskilled children and young people and illiterate adults. Governments and communities are increasingly apprehensive about the social dangers resulting from the increasing number of ghettos of poverty, unemployment, crime and under-education in their midst.

Education for all is not only a moral obligation and a right, it is also an investment with very high potential rates of individual and social return. Hence a growing readiness integrate policies and expenditures on education into the heartland of national development plans and development strategies.

However, these strategic plans and programmes, over several decades, have not succeeded in eliminating major inequities and patterns of exclusion even in the economically most advanced countries. Nor have they generally attempted to cover the whole gamut of priorities identified in the EFA programme, although it is increasingly realised that basic education means inclusive, comprehensive and coherent policies of lifelong learning for all. The difficulties facing countries as they move towards fully inclusive education are often enormous. Not everything can be done on a short time scale but there should be well defined strategies and action programmes that demonstrably and over time will diminish where they cannot entirely eliminate the present massive inequities.

As the previous chapters have shown exclusion, for one reason or another, occurs at all stages, from early childhood to adult education. Despite significant progress, the exclusion of girls and other widespread inequities are still on a very large scale. Substantial, within-country inequalities resulting from geographical location, gender, socio-economic class, cultural background, health and fitness continue. While some groups are privileged to receive a sound education from infancy to higher education, others are in dire poverty and distress, having little or no opportunity and access at all. The application of a blanket policy, target or priority—for example 'to reduce adult illiteracy rates', or 'make more extensive provision of early childhood education and care'—can have the paradoxical effect that more education (for some) increases rather than diminishes inequality. As a corollary, more education can sometimes result in high levels of social and economic inefficiency as a result of concentration of resources on the few to the effective exclusion of the many. This is in direct contravention of the Jomtien Declaration. It is not enough simply to call for extra resources: they must be very carefully targeted ad there must be demonstrable efficiency in their management and use.

The Jomtien decade has witnessed substantial and highly significant gains in access and participation and in certain equity measures (e.g. universal participation in primary education). Closer analysis of the data reveals continuing, sometimes increasing, inequitable provision and practice, Indeed, the problem has grown.

A much better balance is needed: ensuring a fair share of resources and opportunities for all people not just those within easy reach of the centres of power or well placed to take advantage of what is on offer. Respecting and providing for individual differences and circumstances does not excuse highly differentiated policies that in some cases are actually increasing inequality. The same for all can mean greater inequity: those who have least need more, and they need the kind of support and encouragement that enables them to enter the gallery of learning and proceed successfully along its passageways. It is manifestly the case that no society is achieving this degree of equity but it is no less true that in adopting the Jomtien target countries are committed to moving, and moving sharply, in this direction. Movement there certainly has been, sometimes against appalling odds, but the target remains a very powerful challenge for Dakar and beyond.

The two major impediments to equity identified in the EFA 2000 Assessments are poverty and cultural attitudes. To this might be added shortcomings in policies and the lack of readiness and ability to work effectively in achieving targets. People in the direst straits of poverty may very well understand the need for, say, early childhood education, literacy and an educational awakening for girls, but lack the means to act. Communities, regions and whole countries are also in this predicament. Conversely, poverty can stand in the way of a realisation of the need for and value of education. This compounds those cultural attitudes which are hostile to the education of girls, for example, or indifferent to the needs of the excluded. Where resources are extremely scarce, tradition often dictates that boys will get the lion's share. Other considerations come into play: a country needs highly trained elites but undue concentration of resources there is likely to reinforce not diminish existing inequities.

There are other impediments: social infrastructure; lack of responsible leadership; the quality and effectiveness of administrations and the availability of trained personnel are also barriers to equity. The problems may not be 'perceived' or are not treated seriously—or there may be a reluctance to engage with voluntary bodies and local communities in working on these issues. Change is neither rapid nor easy, but results achieved in many countries, not always those best placed—show that it is possible. The issue is, having declared the equity goal and set in motion a decade of activity, how best to set new targets and priorities and mobilise public and private resources to address the outstanding gaps and weaknesses, so that education becomes both better and fairer.

QUALITY, RELEVANCE AND EFFECTIVENESS

As noted in the discussion above of the target dimension on improving the quality of learning, the EFA 2000 Assessment include relatively little data on qualitative improvements in learning by children, youth and adults. The primary concerns in many countries have been meeting quantitative targets of enrolment and progression, yet there have been many expressions of concern about the quality of provision, teaching and learning. These are increasing and will require action on many fronts.

Data sources within countries and internationally that throw light on the quality of learning and teaching and standards of attainment are scattered variable. It would require a major research effort to gather and analyse the necessary material. Many countries already have or are taking steps to establish national assessments, testing schemes and a strong role for school inspectors. Many, however, do not have adequate procedures for quality assurance. Or, if they do, the regular monitoring of results and interpretation of the is not seen as a high priority. The international debate on educational quality, relevance and effectiveness is being conducted, often on a narrow range of topics and commonly on an extremely limited empirical basis.

What is evident, however, is that the huge efforts and resources being deployed to make quantitative gains have yet to be matched in large parts of the world by equal attention to the quality of teaching, learning, facilities and resources. Many of the reports speak with feeling about very basic requirements which are not being met in some countries and regions within them-South Asia and Sub-Saharan Africa, for example. By contrast, in richer regions and countries learning facilities and resources can be quite lavish at least for some sections of the population. It does not follow that a high quality of educational experience results. One indicator of this is the performance of countries in the Third International Science Study.

The quality of the learning experience is not precisely dependent on the richness of the environment, but there are widely agreed limitations—such as very high student-staff ratios, ill-educated and untrained teachers, and lack of the most rudimentary classroom resources for reading and writing.

Learners have a key role in identifying the relevance and quality of their own learning (and teaching) in their terms. There need to be better connections between learner expectations and the standards being set. Quality of learning is highly variable and, for many, quite low. The EFA 2000 Assessments indicate a wide range—from high quality effective education in many countries to a very inadequate standard in others. No less important, within-country differences are marked, sometimes quite extreme. The widespread use of tests and examinations that do nothing to enhance creativity, initiative, problem solving capacity, team work, judgement and other qualities much in need in contemporary life is a barrier to improved quality. Paradoxically they are usually treated as quality measures, as well as screening devices.

The issue of relevance is quite contentious in that what is highly relevant and important for one group may be of little interest to another. In the reports, two main issues emerge: the suitability of educational content and processes in preparing children and youth for work and social responsibility; and the matching of educational provision and resources to specific groups and individuals. In the economically advanced countries, especially, there has been a constant succession of initiatives to tie educational goals and practices more closely to the changing employment market, and to find ways of integrating adults into economic life. For many former colonial countries the issue that has been pinpointed is to find ways to match education better to local requirements.

But while the reports identify specific weaknesses and needs, they do not provide the means to assess and draw conclusions about changes in the quality, relevance and effectiveness of learning. For the future, new and more incisive ways will have to be found, both to bring about the improvements that are widely sought and to provide convincing, publicly acceptable accounts of just what improvements-or setbacks-are actually occurring.

In the final analysis, improvements that are widely sought in the effectiveness, quality and relevance of basic education cannot be achieved short of major changes in the conditions of teaching, teacher education and teacher professionalism. When surveys show, in Sub-Saharan Africa, that the majority of teachers would prefer to change occupations, it is time to question the conditions of teachers' work and the rewards and incentives available to them. The subject of the educational standards of the teaching force is as serious as the lack of supply or the ability or willingness to fund large increases in recruitment and training. Many reports point to very low status and salaries—a rare exception is Fiji where following a Job Evaluation Review of the public Sector in 1998, teaching has become one of the highest paid jobs in the civil service, with incentive allowances for rural postings and regular cost-of-living adjustments.

There is a cruel irony in a large number of countries in the triangular relationship of : the highest aspirations for educational reform; needs of learners; and the quantity, quality, status and remuneration of teachers. There are several trade-offs: higher enrolments and the employment of untrained and poorly paid teachers who are yet of insufficient number to hold pupil-teacher ratios down—or improved student-teacher ratios but no salary increase. Or higher earnings by teachers, but at the cost of having to hold down a second or even third job.

The issue of improvements in the educational quality gave rise in the reports to only a small number of proposals on teaching beyond better training and deployment of more teachers in deprived areas. By contrast, in some countries and especially in the European region, employers' organisations are calling for a radical restructuring of the teaching profession: greater differential of salaries, performance pay, short term contracts, competition among (self-managed) schools and more exacting standards for entry into the profession. Whether moves in these directions or the retention of the more bureaucratic and centralised system of teacher employment typical of most countries would give better results in the quality of student learning is likely to become a hotly debated subject as the trend towards performance appraisal—of teacher as well as students—intensifies.

SHARING RESPONSIBILITY

Two aspects of sharing responsibility arise from the Jomtien experience of the EFA movement. The first aspect is the concept of EFa as itself a partnership of countries, intergovernment organisations, NGOs and others. The second is the grassroots movements of community participation including people and groups taking responsibility for their own education and development, working very often in close association with NGOs and government authorities which increasingly are devolving traditionally centralised roles and responsibilities.

Taking the first aspect, the EFA movement as itself a partnership, it can be seen that in consequence of the decision at Jomtien to ground the EFA movement in learning and development, in education rather than schooling, responsibility for action has been shared by quite different parties. Thus, there as been a partnership for the design, steering and implementation of the overall EFA programme. The international agencies have sponsored, financed or undertaken projects, individually and collectively. A large number of NGOs have contributed by supporting and undertaking projects either directly related to or within the broad policy umbrella of the Jomtien Framework for Action. Ministries of education, health, agriculture and others have mounted special projects and monitored changes in accordance with the directions set at Jomtien. Individual experts, research agencies and others have carried out surveys and evaluations and produced reports. The EFA Forum is a major international collaborative efforts of international interchange, policy discussion, negotiation and purposive action. Overall, this has the character of a loosely coupled coalition but within it there have been powerful and effective partnerships with and within countries to effect change.

The preparation of the draft Framework for Action and the implementation of the decisions and agreements at Dakar will be the responsibility of several international organisations, governments, agencies and NGOs. Monitoring and reporting of progress during the Jomtien decade has been shared by these organisations and others including donor agencies. This can be counted as an effective partnership in that the necessary breadth and cohesiveness of the programme adopted in 1990 has been sustained throughout the Jomtien decade. Behind this general observation, however, lies a considerable variation in effective involvement and support. The decline in donor agency funding means that Jomtien expectations in that respect were not fully met, although the recovery in the late 90s is to be welcomed. International co-operation at the programme level has certainly occurred, both through collaborative efforts among the intergovernmental and non-governmental organisations, and among professionals across countries. The results of all this are not easy to trace, since they are scattered and have not been systematically collated. That is less important than that there has been action, but for the future better monitoring and reporting of how responsibilities are being shared and the synergies that occur would be most useful. This is important for mobilising public opinion as well as professional engagement.

Taken as a whole, the reports and statistical tables have yielded information and provided insights into many aspects of learning and the conditions affecting them, which would have been beyond the capacity of any single agency or organisation to orchestrate. The exercise of the management role by the EFA Forum Secretariat has resulted in a comprehensively documented programme on a very large scale and of major international significance. On the other hand, it has been easier to produce findings on formal structures, especially primary schools, than on informal education and on the several aspects of human development and conditions affecting it that were agreed at Jomtien to be the subject of sustained action and study.

If the Dakar decision is to continue EFA as a broad-based, multi-dimensional, worldwide programme on the enhancement of learning and education, further consideration will need to be given to ways that the international partners can best collaborate and work with countries, agencies, NGOs and others to ensure comprehensive and balanced coverage of all dimensions. There may be need, for example, to draw in other partners if a breadth of coverage similar to that sought at Jomtien is envisaged. For example, major 'consumers' of education are employers and professional bodies. Their views on the quality and relevance of educational outcomes need to be heard. The concepts of 'development education' and 'education for development' need to be revitalised, so that they are seen to be of more direct relevance to all countries regardless of their level of economic development. The Jomtien partnership, for example, did not sufficiently engage a considerable number of the most advanced economies presumably because they believed it to be relevant only to their donor roles.

The partnerships and shared responsibilities for the next decade will require careful initial planning to ensure that all the interests are engaged and see the relevance of internationally collaborative work and shared responsibility. Thus the partnership concept needs to be examined with reference to those countries and parts of countries that, while signatories at Jomtien, have not provided reports. Several of the target directions apply to all countries, regardless of their level of development. A consequence of the relative paucity of reports from industralised countries, for example, is that the experience of some of the world's most advanced educational systems has not been shared. A more effective global partnership would ensue on their more active participation.

The interests and requirements of all countries have to be brought into play so that a global partnership is fully achieved. One of these requirements from the perspective of several non-participating countries, is likely to be a practical set of intermediate goals and more manageable ways of monitoring and assessing progress in areas where qualitative judgement is appropriate. Although some of the directions are of little domestic concern to a number of countries, others are of direct interest: low quality; variable standards; adult literacy; employment skills; social cohesion and others. Countries could perhaps be encouraged to make more selective use of targets, focusing on those most relevant to them. Also, there is scope for widening the range of intergovernmental organisations taking part in the Forum.

There is a growing realisation of the need for more cohesiveness across different policy areas. The Jomtien decade has demonstrated the interrelatedness of education, child-care, health, welfare, employment, finance and other major policy domains. But not all of these sectors have been actively or effectively involved. Better working relations across and within separate ministries and agencies are needed if this cohesiveness is to be achieved in practice. There are some examples of this, notably in the cross-sectoral strategies directed at disadvantaged groups and areas, for the purpose of creating a critical mass of linked interventions in solving obdurate community problems. There is scope for more and better inter-ministerial collaboration.

The second aspect of the issue of shared responsibility is the move by central governments in many countries to devolve several of their powers and roles to regions, states and communities. The active engagement of NGOs and donor bodies and private providers among others has meant a shifting pattern of sometimes quite complex relations between them and different levels and areas of government. Some of the reports allude to difficulties, including unproductive competition and duplication of effort. There is, also, widespread concern that the devolution of financial responsibility can mean a dislocation of budgetary arrangements and a decrease in revenues.

However, an important shift is occurring around the world, whereby the old model of detailed control, management and funding by central ministries is being replaced by more strategic roles and functions for the centre and quite varied networks of decision-making, governance and management, often at a very local level. The sense of ownership and control by local communities, and of people taking responsibility for their own destiny can be a major factor in the success of programmes, as for example in the grass roots literacy campaigns in India in the early 90s. The need for articulation of national roles and responsibilities with the grass roots endeavours was also shown in the Indian experience. Local decision-making also needs to be such that it does not result in growing inequalities among different communities.

More private providers, more partnerships between industry and public sector institutions and bodies and more parental involvement means that new, more participatory management and leadership skills are required. This awakening of civil society has major implications for democratic government and for the content and processes of education. (25) Children as well as adults need to learn to be more responsible for social affairs and more capable of mobilising resources in pursuit of shared community goals. They also need to show initiative and entrepreneurship and be independent.

The exercise of choice is proving a contentious issue in some countries when applied to choice of school, but it is clear that the broad movements of devolved decision-making, partnerships and cross-sectoral collaboration will require a greatly enhanced and diffused capacity to weigh options and make decisions. The sharing of responsibility has emerged in the course of the 90s as an issue of considerable complexity and increasing importance.

New steering mechanisms are being put in place but it is questionable whether governments anywhere have developed structures and strategies sufficient to meet the new challenges. Modalities of partnership are still evolving, not without tension.

Teachers and their professional organisations are often uneasy about what might be meant for their responsibilities and status Parents are often a loss to know what is expected of them (apart from financial contributions) and how to play new roles in school level decision making. The concept of shared responsibility is still being worked out and needs to be made effective as a means of advancing EFA.

MOBILISING RESOURCES

A constant, pervasive theme in all of the EFA 2000 Assessment reports is the inadequacy of resources available to meet what are quite often very basic requirements. This plea is heard not only in poorer countries, but also in some richer countries as an explanation for unequal conditions and provision or unfunded programmes. Resources are always short in relation to demand so the issue becomes one of priorities and efficiency: more jet planes or more primary school places; more places in higher education or more adult literacy campaigns. What distinguishes the high achieving countries? A general answer is the mix of high levels of both public and private expenditure, combined with close attention to resource management and efficiency.

The Jomtien agenda helped set priorities and stimulated a great deal of programme activity. On the evidence available it is slowly gaining ground by way of generating major efficiency gains – improvements in repetition rates and over-age enrolments in primary schools, for example.

The reductions in donor funding that occurred in the wealthier countries through much of the 90s were in a context where many donor and recipient countries alike were experiencing changes in fiscal policies and structural adjustment programmes designed to reduce public debt and contain levels of government expenditures. The restoration of aid budgets in the late 90s, if only to the levels of the beginning of the decade and the debt relief decisions now being taken by several OEFD countries, are important contributions to capacity building and educational development in some of the countries that have had the greatest difficulty in following the Jomtien agenda.

Some national reports document extensive aid programmes in the form of both public funding and community action. For example, the Japanese national report includes an account of a wide range of measures to support EFA targets in other countries: through the Asian Programme for Educational Innovation and Development including associated specified centres in Japan, the Asia-Pacific Centre for UNESCO literacy support programmes, toward funds to promote literacy and provide training. The work of the National Federation of UNESCO Associations in Japan in the 'Terakoya Movement' fosters and supports grassroots learning centres for the poor and the excluded, especially adult women and girls. Donor Support for the development of capacity is extremely important and is comprehensively documented in the thematic study on this subject. NGO roles are varied – contributing material and human resources – extensive, and are highly commended in many reports.

Education expenditure as a share of GDP in several countries shows upward growth; in others it has not always been maintained let alone increased in line with Jomtien targets. In Countries in Transition, public resources for education are now far less than in 1990 and they are being divided less equally. Countries that have experienced decline include Bulgaria, Hungary and Slovenia. While others have maintained or increased the share (the Czech Republic, Lithuania, Poland and Russia for example) the public budget has been greatly diminished. Spending decreased in real terms from 25 to 75 per cent in countries where data are available – for example by 33 per cent in Russia, 47 per cent in Lithuania and 75 per cent in Bulgaira. Devolution by central government of financial responsibility to regions and calls for additional private sources of finance are leading to widening differentiation in per capita expenditure. School conditions in conflict regions in South Eastern Europe have deteriorated drastically. This condition, together with refugee movements will require massive injection of finance just to make up lost ground (26).

The resource issue is not simply one of how governments can acquire additional finance and allocate it to educational spending. Broad education and fiscal reform need to go hand in hand. There has been a steady move to diversify funding sources, a corollary to the principle of sharing responsibility for governance and decision-making. Families and local communities are expected to contribute more and industry and commerce are called on to contribute directly especially to adult education and training or to make some of their facilities and equipment available for educational purposes. The evidence, however, is that many families and communities lack the capacity to take on additional financial burdens. Great care is needed with devolved financial responsibility and the increased reliance on private sources of funding. Many commentators have noted the risk of reduced levels of public funding. Measures are needed to ensure that devolution does not exacerbate existing inequalities between communities, districts and other local entities. This issue has received less attention in the reports than it deserves. It will necessarily feature in any further work.

Alongside the diversification of funding sources is the drive to make more efficient use of funds and of physical plant, facilities and equipment, including shared use of a variety of community resources. The argument for increased resources is often countered by the claim that there is insufficient effort being made to increase efficiency and use resources more intensively and creatively. The reports do provide examples of improvisation, multiple use of facilities and cost saving. Several of the thematic studies point to actual or possible economies, for example use of the cheaper rather than more expensive media where there is no evidence that learning would be improved by the more costly option. However, there would be value in more systematic reporting of how resources are being more effectively used including better use of the public media to publicise these gains.

Issues to address include the proportion of national resources devoted to education, levels of expenditure per pupil, the impact of fees and other charges not only on families but on levels of public funding. But no less important are measures to manage resources efficiently and to gain the maximum educational benefit for the least expenditure of funds for which there will always be too many demands. Few of the reports dealt in any depth with these issues, tending to concentrate instead on overall poverty levels, constraints on budgets and disproportions in the allocation in the resources. Future reporting will benefit from a broader analysis of the resource issue.

Resources of course are not only financial and material. By general consent the key resource is human, whether parent, family member, neighbour, teacher, health worker, community developer, aid worker or technical specialist.

The scope, scale, content and organisation of professional training and development have not been treated systematically in the EFA 200 Assessment although there are statistical data to build on for future work. Resource questions will continue to loom large in the next phase of EFA. Due not least to the advances that have been made in reaching the minimum Jomtien targets for access and participation, human resources and their development will require more intensive treatment and analysis in the decade ahead.

TOWARDS A NEW KNOWLEDGE BASE

There have been striking and highly commendable qualitative and quantitative contributions of the EFA 2000 Assessment to the international knowledge base. Self-evaluation based on extensive data sets has been a feature of many national reports and all of the regional syntheses. Knowledge and understanding of what is being done, what needs to be done and how to make further progress have markedly improved. We have a better knowledge of problems, of where they are and what needs to be done to solve them. A global education indicators system has been produced despite the many difficulties encountered in gathering and verifying data. While serious gaps remain, this and preceding work to improve the international education statistics serve as foundations for developments and refinements which over time will greatly improve understanding and decision-making.

Through the co-ordinated efforts to provide useable data, countries previously lacking necessary structures and techniques have improved their own capability and learnt a great deal about how their own systems are functioning, while others with advanced systems have shared their expertise and experience and improved their level of international understanding. There has been collaboration among international organisations of which the joint work of UNESCO and OECD in producing world education indicators is an example. All this could be taken much further.

For continuing progress, there must be a greater investment including assistance and advice to countries with support not only at the national level but at regional and local levels as well. The value of district level data gathering and analysis is well illustrated in the studies and maps produced in the South and East Asia region. There are some remarkable examples of highly localised information gathering and processing in India, leading to action programmes. Gathering and anaylsing data is a costly business. Judgements will be required about what will be most useful, for decision-makers and for purposes of transparency and public accountability.

Many aspects of EFA are not susceptible to representation through indicators.? As the OECD experience demonstrates, a long and costly process is required to produce a comprehensive, sound international education indicators system. The OECD system still, after more than a decade of intensive and expensive development work involving the specialist staff of statistical agencies in member countries, includes only a relatively small amount of data on outputs and concerns of only 29 countries. Other and much more varied sources of information have to be drawn on in making judgements about the performance and quality of educational systems. These sources include inspection systems, commissioned research, evaluation studies tests and other assessments of students, expert committees, conferences, polls and censuses, the assembling of information and ideas from partners and interested parties, and anecdotal evidence.

Many of these and other sources are already in use in countries as part of a continuing process of gathering, filtering and applying knowledge. The days of inadequate briefings for ministers and policy makers and decisions uninformed by data and knowledge may not have entirely passed, but they are numbered as the information society becomes ever more a reality. Advances in technology, research methodology and the training of analysts have resulted in a vast increase in educational knowledge and access to data.

These developments, however, have increased the gap between those countries, regions and groups of people with the ability to generate and access educational knowledge and the rest. Regrettably, a number of countries highly advanced in this respect have not contributed data to the EFA 2000 Assessment whereas some countries with slender resources and weak systems have rallied to the leadership provided through the regional EFA networks. Particularly impressive is the progress work through the preparation of the regional and sub-regional synthesis in the Asia-Pacific region. For the future, further development of this kind of capacity building, the direct involvement of all the knowledge-rich countries and greater use of their expertise will strengthen the international endeavour to generate and apply educational knowledge.

The combined effort of all the players has shown what is possible and what is still needed.

- more systematic data gathering and analysis to strengthen the indicators system, making it more accurate and usable including its potential for trend analysis;
- further study of ways of ascertaining changing patterns of behaviour and the impact of different educational policies on specific target areas;

- selection of key issues and topics to be illuminated by special studies both quantitative and qualitative and drawing on the highest levels of international expertise;
- encouragement to governments, donors, and others with programme and project responsibilities to build evaluation into initial designs and to produce and widely disseminate reports on results and how they were achieved, using multi-media not just printed documents;
- advanced training programmes and assistance to countries in need of improved systems for monitoring and evaluation;
- studies on the strategic role of educational knowledge in informing policy-making in the emerging knowledge-based society;
- advice and assistance to the increasing numbers and greater diversity of decision-makers at regional and local levels on ways to improve their educational knowledge, monitor activities and use feedback;
- streamlining international mechanisms for regular monitoring and evaluating major programmes as they progress, with feedback to participating countries and agencies.

WHAT DIFFERENCE IS EFA MAKING?

Did Jomtien make a difference? If so, to whom and for what reasons? These are questions which will be debated at Dakar where a multiplicity of answers will be given. They are also addressed, directly or indirectly, in the numerous reports that have been produced for the EFA 2000 Assessment Ministers, donors, NGOs and individual experts will have their own answers. This

Global Synthesis has attempted to draw up a balance sheet of what worked and what did not, but there are too many imponderables and too many gaps in the data for simple conclusions to be drawn. However, the following are undoubtedly achievements which if only partially attributable to the EFA movement, nevertheless have either been stimulated and fostered by it, or have helped to consolidate and strengthen it:

- Significant improvements in achieving enrolment and participation targets and at all levels of education including early childhood care and education;
- Big reduction in some countries in inequities, notably in the area of gender, disability and ethnic minorities;
- Big reductions in a small number of countries in volumes and/or rates of adult illiteracy;
- New policies, frameworks, legislation and resources in some countries to pursue one or more of the EFA target directions;
- Greater involvement of non-government organistions, community groups and parents in decision making, action programmes and the operation of child care and education facilities;
- Big improvements in educational information and in analytic and evaluative capacity (the knowledge base);
- The targets, although not achieved or fully achieved, are more attainable than a decade ago.

Would none of this have occurred had the World Declaration not been made and the Framework for Action adopted in Jomtien in 1990? The answer cannot be certain. Doubtless much of it would have happened, since existing policies and programmes were being built on—not displaced—but in more piecemeal ways, without the sense of international commitment, drive and cooperative endeavour, and it would not have been documented and analysed for purposes of a further commitment and renewal of effort. There is evidence of actions taken on a very large number of countries to implement the Jomtien agenda and many have been successful.

What was not achieved? None of the targets has been fully achieved; for some, though, there has been great progress. In some regions there have been major setbacks, including declines, for example in enrolment and participation in primary schooling, gender equity and meeting the needs of socially disadvantaged groups. On the one hand, targets could be described as over-ambitious, even quite unrealistic for some countries. But, on the other hand, setting ambitious targets is a means of stirring up inertia and mobilising efforts and resources. In several situations there has been a failure of governments and agencies to respond adequately to people's needs; in others, administrations have not met the requirements even when the policy commitment has been strong.

It is a sign of strength, not weakness, that failures, setbacks and shortcomings are so freely admitted and discussed. This bodes well for the future.

The Jomtien movement cannot be judged a failure simply because targets have not been achieved although that must be of great concern when little or no progress has been made. Worse, there have been serious losses. What is important, however, is to reach a conclusion about whether the effort has been worthwhile, whether sufficient commitment, energy and resourcefulness have been present, and whether there is value in taking the next step. The answer yielded by this Global Synthesis is that the effort has been worthwhile, indeed necessary, and that the mission of EFA must again be taken up, with strengthened resolve and renewed energy. Too much is at stake for anything less.

Towards More Equitable Education

Equity does not imply precisely equal provision nor does it entail a mathematical equality of outcomes. People, their interests, needs, and circumstances differ too much for that. Instead, equitable education for all requires:

- that all are engaged in the process and are given equal consideration;
- that the opportunities, facilities and programmes appropriate to their specific needs and requirements off all people are available and used;
- that the learning programmes undertaken and their outcomes are of an equivalent value and use to all individuals and society.

Spending Patterns

A UNICEF study of 10 developing countries that universalised primary schooling early in the development process and then increased secondary enrolments identified common features in spending patterns:

- public expenditure on education represented a high share of GDP and of total public expenditure;
- a higher expenditure per pupil as a percentage of GNP per capita and a lower one in higher education than comparable countries;
- measures were taken to keep unit costs low and internal efficiency high;
- minimum quality standards were maintained while enrolments expanded;
- costs to parents were mostly reduced.

Source: Mehrotra, S. Education for All: Policy Lessons from High Achieving Countries; Siniscalco, M.T. Achieving Education for All: Demographic Challenges

Contd...

In **South and East Africa**, governments have adopted measures to contain costs:

- tax and other incentives to the private sector for supporting primary education;
- distance and mobile education, Q'ranic schools and other complementary services;
- double shifts;
- more intensive use of text books and book rental;
- increasing internal efficiency e.g. grade promotion;
- greater involvement of civil society through decentralisation.

Source : **Draft Regional Synthesis—South and East Africa**

References

1. BRAY, M. 2000. *Community Partnerships in Education: Dimensions, Variations, and Implications*. Thematic study for the EFA 2000 Assessment. EFA Forum in Association with the World Bank.

   MONTAGNES, I. 1999. *Textbooks and Learning Materials 1990–1999: A Global Survey*. Thematic study for the EFA 2000 Assessment. EFA Forum in association with DfID

   PERRATON, H. AND CREED, C. 2000. *Applying New Technologies and Cost-Effective Delivery Systems in Basic Education.* Thematic study of the EFA 200 Assessment. EFA Forum in association with DfID.

   ROBINSON, C. 2000. Partnerships in Education for All – NGO and Civil Society Experiences. The Collective Consultation of NGOs on Literacy and Education for All. In: *Renewed Hope: NGOs and Civil Society in Education for All.* Thematic Study for the EFA 2000 Assessment EFA Forum in association with UNESCO.

2. J. Delors et al. 1996. *Learning: The Treasure Within. Report to UNESCO of the International Commission on Education for the Twenty-first Century*, Paris, UNESCO Publishing, 1996.

3. *Framework for Action – Meeting Basic Learning Needs. Guidelines for implementing the World Declaration on Education for All.* Jomtien Thailand, 5–9 March 1990.

4. WHITMAN, C.V., LEVINGER, B., ALDINGER, C., BIRDTHISTLE, I., JONES, J. 2000. *School Health and Nutrition.* (Executive Summary). Thematic study for the EFA 2000 Assessment. EFA Forum in association with WHO.

5. *A Synthesis Report of Education for All 2000 Assessment in the East and South East Asia Sub-Region.* Working Paper No. 2. By K. Vine Bangkok. UNESCO Principal Regional Office for Asia and the Pacific, January 2000. p. 22.

6. *Education at a Glance. The OECD Education Indicators.* Paris, OECD. (1998)

7. BERNARD, A.K. 1999. *Education for All and Children who are Excluded.* Thematic study for the EFA 2000 Assessment EFA Forum in association with UNICEF. (October 25. 1st draft).

   BOTH, T 2000. *Inclusion in Education: Participation of Disabled Learners.* Thematic study for the EFA 2000 Assessment. EFA Forum in association with UNESCO.

8. SINISCALCO, M. T. 2000. *Achieving Education for All: Demographic Challenges* (draft manuscript). Thematic study of the EFA 2000 Assessment. EFA Forum in association with UNESCO

9. MILLER, E. 2000. *Education in the Caribbean in the 1900s: Retrospect and Prospect*: Education for All in the Caribbean: Assessment 2000 Monograph Series. UNESCO. p. 10.

10. ABLETT, J. and SLENGESOL, I-A. 2000. *Education in Crisis: The Impact and Lessons of the East Asian Financial Shock, 1997–1999.* (6 January draft). Thematic study for the EFA 2000 Assessment. EFA Forum in association with the World Bank.

11. *Education in Emergencies and for Reconstruction.* New York. UNICEF. 1999.

12. *Final Report 5th International Conference on Adult Education. Hamburg Germany. 14-18 July 1997.* Paris. UNESCO. 1997.

13. WAGNER, D. 2000. Literacy and Adult Education. (Executive Summary). Thematic study for the EFA 2000 Assessment. EFA Forum in association with UNESCO.

14. CHINA. *Education for All: The Year 2000 Assessment Final Country Report of China. Beijing.* Chinese National Commission for UNESCO. 1999.

15. WAGNER, D. 2000. *Literacy and Adult Education.* (Executive Summary). Thematic study for the EFA 2000 Assessment. EFA Forum in association with UNESCO.

16. MATHEW, A. 1999. *Strides in Education for All. Non-formal Adult Education in India.* New Delhi. UNESCO.

17. *Performance Standards in Education. In Search of Quality.* Paris, OECD. 1995

18. HUMAN SCIENCES RESEARCH COUNCIL. 1999. *With Africa for Africa: Towards Quality Education for All.* CHINAPAH, V. (ed). Education for All 2000 Assessment Survey. 1999 MLA Project. Draft Regional Report. Pretoria.

AL NHAR, T. 2000. *Learning Achievement of Grade Four Elementory Students in Some Arab Countries. Regional Report.* Beirut. UNESCO Regional Office for Education in the Arab States.

KAZAKHSTAN. 1999. *Monitoring Learning Achievements* Kazakhstan. UNESCO Almaty.

LATIN AMERICAN EDUCATIONAL QUALITY ASSESSMENT LABORATORY. 1998. *First International Comparative Study of Language, Mathematics, and Associated Factors in Third and Fourth Grades.* Santiago. UNESCO

19. SINISCALCO, M.T. 2000 *Achieving Education for All: Demographic Challenges.* (draft manuscript). Thematic study for the EFA 2000 Assessment. EFA Forum in association with UNESCO.

20. SCHWARTZMAN, S. 20000. *Education for All: the Nine Largest Countries.* Version March 17. E-9 conference 2000. Regional report of the EFA 2000 Assessment.

21. *A Synthesis Report of Education for All 2000 Assessment for the Asia-Pacific Region.* Working Paper No. 2. By K. Vine and V Ordonez. Bangkok. UNESCO Principal Regional Office for Asia and the Pacific January, 2000. p. 11.

22. *Education for All in the Arab States: a Renewed Commitment. The Arab Framework for Action to Meet Basic Learning Needs in the Years 2000-2015.* Preliminary Draft no 1. UNESCO Regional Office for Education in the Arab States. January 2000. p. 11

23. *Preparing Youth for the 21st Century. The Transition from Education to the Labour Market.* Paris. OECD. 1999.

24. *Thematic Review of the Transition from Initial Education to Working Lif.* Paris. OECD. (in press).

25. BELLAH, R. N. et al 1992 *The Good Society. New York Vintage Books.*

26. MOTIVANS, A, 2000. *Education for All – Central and Eastern Europe Synthesis Report.* UNESCO Institute for Statistics/ UNICEF Innocent Research Centre. Regional report for the EFA 2000 Assessment.

Sources

1. EFA INTERNATIONAL CONSULTATIVE FORUM DOCUMENTS

The Dakar Framework for Action: Education for All. Meeting Our Collective Commitments. 3rd draft. Paris. EFA Forum.

MELLOR, W. *EFA 2000 Assessment Thematic Studies.* Authors and Author Outlines. 23 February 2000.

EFA Statistical Documet (in progress) UNESCO Institute for Statistics. Paris.

Framework for Action – Meeting Basic Learning Needs. Guidelines for Implementing the World Declaration on Education for All. Jomtien Thailand,5-9 March 1990.

Education for All: the Year 2000 Assessment. Technical Guildelines. Paris. EFA Forum. UNESCO.

LITTLE, A. and MILLER, E. 2000 *The International Consultative Forum on Education for All 1990 – 2000. An Evaluation.* A draft discussion document to the EFA Forum Steering Committee meeting February 2000.

MELLOR, W. *Tasks and Milestones for EFA Thematic Studies.* Thematic Studies—Tasks, Timelines and Coordination. 23 February 2000.

World Declaration on Educaiton for All – Meeting Basic Learning Needs. Jomtien Thailnand 5-9 March, 1990.

World Declaration on Educaiton for All and Framework for Action to Meet Basic Learning Needs. The Amman Affirmation. World Confernece on Education for All. Jomtien Thailand.5-9 March 1990.

2. EFA REGIONAL REPORTS

A) Arab States and North Africa

AL NHAR, T. 2000. *Learning Achievement of Grade Four Elementary Students in Some Arab Countries Regional Report.* Beirut. UNESCO Regional Office for Education in the Arab States.

Education for All in the Arab States: a Renewed Commitment. The Arab Framework for Action to Meet Basic Learning Needs in the Years 2000-2015. Preliminary Draft no. 1. UNESCO Regional Office for Education in the Arab States. January 2000.

Education for All in the Arab States Assessment 2000. Regional Report. Executive Summary. UNESCO Regional Office for Education in the Arab States. January 2000.

B) Asia and Pacific

Tripartite Evaluation Report. Extra-Budgetary Activities funded by Governments of Japan and Norway. Asia-Pacific Programme of Education for All (APPEAL) 1998 Bangkok. UNESCO Principal Regional Office for Asia and the Pacific.

Achievements, Broadened Visions and Renewed Strategies. Asia-Pacific Programme of Education for All (APPEAL) 2000: Bangkok. UNESCO Principal Regional Office for Asia and the Pacific.

Asia and the Pacific Regional Framework for Action: Education for All. Guiding Principles, Specific Goals and Targets for 2015. Revised version.

A Synthesis Report of Education for All 2000 Assessment in the South and West Asia Sub-Region. Working Paper No. 4. Bangkok. UNESCO PROAP. UNESCO Principal Regional Office for Asia and the Pacific 2000.

Contributions of Multilateral and Bilateral Agencies towards Achieving EFA Goals in the Asia-Pacific Region. United Nations Development Programme 2000. Bangkok. UNESCO PROAP.

A Synthesis Report of Education for All 2000 Assessmen in the East and South East Asia Sub-Region. Working Paper No. 2. By K. Vine Bangkok. UNESCO Principal Regional Office for Asia and the Pacific. January 2000.

A Synthesis Report of Education for All 2000 Assessment in the Trans-Caucasus and Central Asia Sub-Region. Working Paper No. 1. By K. Vine. Bangkok. UNESCO Principal Regional Office for Asia and the Pacific, January 2000.

A Synthesis Report of Education for All 2000 Assessment for the Asia-Pacific Region. Working Paper No. 3. By K. Vine and V. Ordonez. Bangkok. UNESCO Principal Regional Office for Asia and the Pacific. January 2000.

C) Europe and North America

Regional Plan of Action (draft). Rev. 6a 25/2/00.

Education for All Regional Conference for Europe and North America. Regional Plan of Action. Warsaw 6-8 February 2000.

MOTIVANS, A. 2000. *Education for All – Central and Eastern Europe Synthesis Report.* UNESCO Institute for Statistics/ UNICEF Innocenti Research Centre. Regional Report for the EFA 2000 Assessment.

SKILBECK, M. 2000. *Education for All. Trends and Issues from an OECD Perspective. Western Europe and North America.* (draft, 12 January). Regional Report for the EFA 2000 Assessment.

VAN WASSENHOVE, G. and MOUSNY, C. 2000. *Education For All.* Warsaw Regional Conference 6-8 Febuary 2000. Conference working document. EFA Forum.

D) E9 Countries (Nine high population countries)

Recife Declaration of E9 Countries Feb. 2. 2000

SCHWARTZMAN, S. *Education for All: the Nine Largest Countries.* Version March 17, 2000. Regional Report for the EFA 2000 Assessment.

E) Latin America and the Caribbean: The Americas

Latin America Sub-regional Report. Education for All – the Year 2000 Assessment. By R. Blanco and E. Trevino. Santiago. UNESCO. 2000.

EFA Plan of Action for the Americas. Santiago. 2000.

JULES, V. and PANNEFLEK, A. 2000 *Education for All in the Caribbean: Assessment 2000. Subregional Synthesis Report.* Vol. 1: Summary. January.

MILLER, E. 2000 *Education in the Caribbean in the 1900s: Retrospect and Prospect.* Education for All in the Caribbean: Assessment 2000 Monograph Series. UNESCO.

F) Sub-Saharan Africa

Draft Regional Synthesis – South and East Africa 1999 Harare. Sept.-Oct.

Education for All – Report from Spanish, Portuguese and French speaking countries. Assessment during the period 1990/2000.

HUMAN SCIENCES RESEARCH COUNCIL 1999. *With Africa for Africa: Towards Quality Education for All.* CHINAPAH, V (ed). Education for All 2000 Assessment Survey. 1999 MLA Project. Draft Regional Report. Pretoria.

3. EFA THEMATIC STUDIES

ABLETT, J. and SLENGESOL, I-A. 2000 *Education in Crisis: The Impact and Lessons of the East Asian Financial Shock, 1997–1999.* (6 January draft). EFA Forum in association with the World Bank. Paris.

BENSALAH, K., SINCLAIR, M., NACER, F.H., COMMISSO, A., BOKHARI, S. 1999 *Education in Situations of Emergency and Crisis.* EFA Forum in association with UNESCO. Paris

BENTALL, C., PEART, E., CARR-HILL, R. and COX, A. (1999) *Funding Agency Contributions to Education for All.* (10 December 1st draft) and Appendix 1. EFA Forum in association with DfID. Paris/London.

BERNARD, A.K. (1999) *Education for All and Children Who are Excluded.* (October 25. 1st draft). EFA Forum in association with UNICEF. Paris/New York.

BOOTH, T. 2000. *Inclusion in Education: Participation of Disabled Learners.* EFA Forum in association with UNESCO. Paris.

BRAY, M. 2000 *Community Partnerships in Education: Dimensions, Variatins, and Impliations.* EFA Forum in association with the World Bank. Paris/Hong Kong.

DEBOUROU, D. 1999 Participatin communautaire: des experiences des organisations non gouvernmentales et de la société civile. The Collective Consultation of NGOs on Literacy and Education for All. Draft. In: *Renewed Hope: NGOs and Civil Society in Education for All.* EFA Forum in association with UNESCO. 15 November. Paris.

JOMMO, B. Gender Dimensions in Education for All: NGO and Civil Society Experiences. The Collective Consultation of NGOs on Literacy and Education for All. Draft. In: *Renewed Hope: NGOs and Civil Society in Education for All.* EFA Forum in association with UNESCO. Paris/Nairobi.

KAHLER, D. 2000 Linking Non-formal Education to Development: NGO Experiences During the Education for All Decade. The Collective Consultation of NGOs on Literacy and Education for All. Draft In: *Renewed Hope: NGOs and Civil Society in Education for All.* EFA Forum in association with UNESCO. Paris/Boston.

MONTAGNES, I. 1999. *Textbooks and Learning Materials 1990 – 1999: a Global Survey.* EFA Forum in association with DfID. Paris/Port Hope.

MYERS, R. G. 2000 *The EFA Global Thematic Review of Early Childhood Care and Development.* Final draft. February 1. EFA Forum in association with UNICEF.

PATEL, I. (1999) Emerging trends in adult literacy policies and practice in Africa and Asia. NGO perspectives. The Collective Consultation of NGOs on Literacy and Education for All. In: *Renewed Hope: NGOs and Civil Society in Education for All.* Draft. EFA Forum in Association with UNESCO. Paris/Mumbai.

PERRATON, H. and CREED, C. (2000) *Applying New Technologies and Cost-Effective Delivery Systems in Basic Education.* EFA Forum in association with DfID. Paris/Cambridge.

ROBINSON, C. Partnerships in Education for All—NGO and Civil Society Experiences. The Collective Consultation of NGOs on Literacy and Education for All. In: *Renewed Hope: NGOs and Civil Society in Education for All.* Draft. EFA Forum in association with UNESCO. Paris/High Wycombe.

SINISCALCO, M.T. 2000. *Achieving Education for All: Demographic Challenges.* Draft. EFA Forum in association with UNESCO.

WAGNER, D. 2000. *Literacy and Adult Education. Executive Summary.* EFA Forum in association with UNESCO. Paris/ Philadelphia.

WHITMAN, C.V., LEVINGER, B., ALDINGER, C., BIRDTHISTLE, I., JONES, J. 2000. *School Health and Nutrition.* (Executive Summary). 2 February, draft EFA Forum in association with WHO. Paris/Geneva.

4. Selected EFA Country Reports

BRAZIL. EFA 2000 *Education for All: Evaluation of the Year 2000. National Report – Brazil.* National co-ordinator Maria Helena Castro. Brasilia. National Institute for Educational Studies and Research.

CHILE. 1999. *Education para Todos: Evaluacion en el Ano 2000. Informe de Chile.* National co-ordinator Juan Eduardo Garcia-Huidobro. Santiago. Ministry of Education. October.

CHINA. *Education for All: The Year 2000 Assessment Final Country Report of China.* National co-ordinator Mr. Zhang Xuezhong, Beijing. Chinese National Commission for UNESCO.

CUBA. 1999. *Educate Your Child – A home and community-based programme of pre-school training for children aged 0-6- Case Study.* Havana. Centro de Referencia LatinoAmericano para la educacion preescolar.

FIJI. *Education for All Country Report – Fiji.* National co-ordinator Isireli Senibulu. Suva. Ministry of Education.

FRANCE. 1999. *Rapport sur l'Education pour Tous – Bilan a l'an 2000.* National co-ordinator Mrs Marie-Paule Belmas, French National Commission for UNESCO. Paris, Ministéré de IÕEducation.

GERMANY. *Education for All: The Year 2000 Assessment. Country Report Germany.* National co-ordinator Mrs Christine Merkel, German Commission for UNESCO. Berlin.

INDIA. *Education for All: The Year 2000 Assessment Report. India.* National co-ordinator Abhimanyu Singh. Ministry of Human Resource Development. New Delhi.

IRELAND. *EFA Report.* National co-ordinator Mrs Mary Dunne. Dublin. Department of Education and Science.

JAPAN. *EFA 2000 Assessment. Country Report: Japan.* National co-ordinator Mr Ryo Watanabe.

NETHERLANDS. *Education for All: The Year 2000 Assessment* National co-ordinator Mr Dick Lageweg, the Netherlands National Commission for UNESCO, in collaboration with Dept of Educational Studies and Consultancy (DESC) of the Nuffic.

NIGERIA. *Education for All: The Year 2000 Assessment. Nigeria.* National co-ordinator M.O.A. Olorufunmi. Abuja. Federal Ministry of Education.

PAPUA NEW GUINEA. *EFA Assessment 2000. Papua New Guinea Report.* National co-ordinator John Josephs. Waigani. Department of Education.

POLAND. *Education for All: The Year 2000Assessment.* National co-ordinator Mr Krzysztof Kafel. Warsaw. Ministry of National Education.

RUSSIAN FEDERATION. *Education for All: An estimation 2000. Russian Federation.* National co-ordinator Mr Alexander. M. Kondakov. Moscow. Ministry of Education.

SENEGAL *Rapport National du Bilan de I'Education Pour Tous en I'an 2000.* National co-ordinator Momar Sow. Dakar. National Ministry of Education.

SOUTH AFRICA. *Education for All: The Year 2000 Assessment. Draft Report.* National co-ordinator Mr N. Mgijma.: Pretoria. National Department of Education.

UNITED KINGDOM. *Education for All: UK Country Report 1999.* National co-ordinator Mr Robert Mace. London. Department for Education and Employment.

UNITED STATES. 2000. *Education for All: A Global Commitment.* National co-ordinator Mr Stephen Moseley. Washington D.C. Academy for Eduational Devleopment.

5. United Nations Agencies

J. Delors et al. 1996 *Learning: The Treasure Within. Report to UNESCO of the International Commission on Education for the Twenty-first Century.* Paris, UNESCO Publishing, 1996.

MEHROTRA, S. 1998. *Education for All: Policy Lessons from High Achieving Countries.* New York. UNICEF.

Final Report 5th International Conference on Adult Education. Hamburg Germany. 14-18 July 1997. Paris. UNESCO. 1997.

Education in Emergencies and for Reconstruction. New York, UNICEF. 1999

World Education Yearbook 2000, Paris, UNESCO. 2000.

World Conference on Higher Education

6. Additional Sources

BELLAH, R. N. et al. 1992. *The Good Society.* New York. Vintage Books.

FISKE, E.B. 1998. *Wasted Opportunities—When Schools Fail.* Education for All Status and Trends. Paris. UNESCO.

FREDERIKSSON, U. 1999. *Education for all Assessment 2000—The teachers' perspective.* Brussels. Septemeber. Education International. Draft synthesis document.

NATIONAL COMMISSION ON EDUCATION 1993. *Learning to Succeed.* London. Heinemann.

Performance Standards in Education. In Search of Quality. Paris, OECD. 1995.

INDIA 1999. *Strides in Education for All. Non-formal Adult Education in India.* By A. Mathew. New Delhi. UNESCO.

Lifelong Learning for All. Paris. OECD. 1996.

JAPAN. *Japanese Partnerships through development of the NFUAJ World Terakoya Movement – Retracing 10 years of history and looking to the futrue.*

Preparing Youth for the 21st Century. The Transition from Education to the Labour Market, Paris. OECD. 1999.

Thematic Review of the Transition from Initial Education to Working Life. Paris. OECD. (in press) *Education at a Glance. The OECD Education Indicators.* Paris. OECD/CERI. 1998.

KAZAKHSTAN. 1999. *Monitoring Learning Achievements* May-June 1999. UNESCO Almaty.

Education Policy Analysis. Paris. OECD/CERI. 1999.

Appendices

1. Interlocutors

Roberto Carneiro, Portugal Christopher Colclough, United Kingdom Helen Connell, Asutralia

John Coolahan, Ireland

Ed Fiske, USA

Phillip Hughes, Australia Warren Mellor, EFA Secretariat

Errol Miller, Jamaica

Tephen Moseley, USA

Christian Nique, France

Colin Power, UNESCO

Sheldon Shaeffer, UNICEF

Maria Teresa Siniscalco, Italy

Gerard van Wassenhove, France

Peter Williams, United Kingdom

2. Reinforcing the Jomtein Message at the International Level

1990 – International Literacy Year

1990 – The World Summit for Children. New York. The first major summit meeting: quality of life; reducing mortality; nutrition; disease; illiteracy; basic education for all children.

1992 – The Conference on Environment and Development. Rio de Janeiro. Role of formal and non-formal education in changing attitudes and understandings re sustainable development. The conference urged governments to implement Jomtien Framework for Action.

1993 – The World Conference on Human Rights. Vienna. Right to development: strive to eradicate illiteracy and humanitarian law, democracy and the role of law, in curricula of all educational institutions.

1933—EFA Summit of the Nine High Population Countries, New Delhi, India.

1994—The International Conference on Population and Development Cairo. Role of education in social change and development; reduction of fertility, morbidity and mortality rates; empowerment of women and closing the gender gap; and improvement in quality of working population.

1995—The Fourth World Conference on Women. Beijing. Education leading to equality, sustainable development and peace; increase girls' enrolment.

1995—The World Summit for Social Development. Conpenhagen. Poverty; unemployment; social exclusion; equal educational opportunities improve educational quality; useful knowledge; reasoning ability; skills; ethical and social values.

1996—The World Food Summit. Rome. The need to meet basic nutritional requirements.

1996—The Mid-Deade Meeting of the International Consultative Forum on Education for All. Amman. Focus on learning—learning and critical thinking to empower individuals to understand changing environments, create new knowledge and shape their own destinies. Education to reinforce mutual respect, social cohesion and democratic governance.

1997—The International Conference on Child Labour. Oslo. Social mobilisation to end the economic exploitation and abuse of children; the interrelationships between child labour and education, in particular the missed educational opportunities.

1997—Fifth International Conference on Adult Education. Hamburg. Active and informed citizenship the key to solving big problems (health hazards, racism, economic crises, ecological hazards).

1998—The First World Conference of Ministers Responsible for Youth Labour.

Lisbon. Lisbon Declaration on Youth, Politics and Programmes calling for governments to strengthen youth policies to ensure active participation of youth in all levels of decision making.

1998 – The Second International Congress on Technical and Vocational Education. Seoul.

In addition, the messages of the International Commission on Education for the Twenty First Century (Delors Report) strongly understood the EFA goals and strategies.